Moments of
Delicate Balance

Selected Poetry by David Lee

Day's Work, 1990
Paragonah Canyon, 1990
My Town, 1995
Covenants (with William Kloefkorn), 1996
Wayburne Pig, 1997
The Fish, 1997
Twenty-one Gun Salute, 1999
A Legacy of Shadow: Selected Poems, 1999
News from Down to the Café: New Poems, 1999
Incident at Thompson Slough, 2002
So Quietly the Earth, 2004

Selected Books by William Kloefkorn

Poetry Collections

Platte Valley Homestead, 1985
Drinking the Tin Cup Dry, 1989
Welcome to Carlos, 2000
Loup River Psalter, 2001
Alvin Turner as Farmer, 2004
Swallowing the Soap, 2010

Short Story Collections

A Time to Sink Her Pretty Little Ship, 1999
Shadow Boxing, 2003

Memoirs

This Death by Drowning, 2001
Restoring the Burnt Child, 2003
At Home on This Moveable Earth, 2006
Breathing in the Fullness of Time, 2009

Moments of Delicate Balance

Part I

William Kloefkorn

Part II

David Lee

WingsPress

San Antonio, Texas
2011

Moments of Delicate Balance
© 2011 by William Kloefkorn and David Lee

Cover image: Photograph by Jan Lee

First Edition

Print Edition ISBN: 978-0-916727-78-9
ePub ISBN: 978-1-60940-123-8
Kindle ISBN: 978-1-60940-124-5
PDF ISBN: 978-1-60940-125-2

Wings Press
627 E. Guenther
San Antonio, Texas 78210
Phone/fax: (210) 271-7805

On-line catalogue and ordering:
www.wingspress.com
All Wings Press titles are distributed to the trade by
Independent Publishers Group
www.ipgbook.com

Library of Congress Cataloging-in-Publication Data:

Kloefkorn, William. 1932-2011.
  Moments of delicate balance / part I, William Kloefkorn ; part II, David Lee.
-- 1st ed.
     p. cm.
  ISBN 978-0-916727-78-9 (pbk. : alk. paper) -- ISBN 978-1-60940-123-8
(ebk.) -- ISBN 978-1-60940-124-5 (Kindle ebk.) -- ISBN 978-1-60940-125-2
(library pdf. ebk.)
  I. Lee, David, 1944 Aug. 13- II. Title.
  PS3561.L626M54 2011
  811'.54--dc22
                                    2011007196

Contents

Part 1 — William Kloefkorn

Part II — David Lee

Part I

William Kloefkorn

for Mary Ann Kloefkorn,
with affection now
as much as then

It is sweet to dance to violins
When Love and Life are fair:
To dance to flutes, to dance to lutes
Is delicate and rare ...

—Oscar Wilde,
  "The Ballad of Reading Gaol"

All the art of living lies
in a fine mingling
of letting go and
holding on.

—Havelock Ellis

After Breakfast at Madonna

—in came the doctor,
in came the nurse,
in came the lady
with the alligator purse.

                                    —anonymous

And in came the rotund priest
with a question on his canonical lips:
Anybody here named Melvin?

Yes, I said, nodding. He's in the bathroom,
in his Buick, brushing his teeth. Look
for yourself. The door is open.

The priest looked. He smiled. I watched
as Melvin finished brushing, watched
as the priest gave my roommate a blessing,

watched as our guest crossed himself
and, in spite of his girth, floated
like an inflated monarch out of the room.

Whereupon.

In came the nurse to wheel Melvin back
to his bed, to guide him atop it,
to tuck him in. When she left, Melvin

turned his head and grinned. All
over his full ruddy face shone the evidence
of salvation. He called me a prick,

and I said Thank you, weakly, because
my lungs were filling again, this time
to overflowing, with corruption.

Almost Spring

The sun is out
and the wind is calm and
the red in the thermometer is rising

and the woman across the street
in the blue sweatshirt
can't stop grinning and

neither can the tyke
in front of her and when he
gathers up the last of the long

winter's snow and packs it
into a ball and throws it
at a robin sitting fat and imperial

in a bush that
like the rest of us can hardly wait
to burst into bloom and

misses it by at least a country mile
I applaud and
Encore! Encore! is what I hear

someone shouting and Hope
wearing only her
birthday apparel appears and

kisses me full on the mouth and
the moment like a curtain
rises and all the world is a stage

and we are on it acting
singly and collectively and gloriously
and god help all of us

forever the insatiable fool.

Angelology

Because I have never seen an angel, because
I have serious doubts that they exist,
I study them seriously,

parse them for what we have named
and given them, orders
to reflect our love

of orders—angels, archangels, principalities,
powers, virtues, dominions,
thrones, cherubim,

seraphim—all of them sporting wings,
all of them male, one
of them now

perched half-human, half-bird on my shoulder,
whispering something I can't
make sense of,

its competition that of a relentless surf,
above it a gull suspended
under a blue sky

patient to yield to a moon that is surely
female, its face akin
to the circle

I drew in first grade, then so painstakingly
colored, my teacher standing
tall beside me,

one hand on my shoulder, Miss Katie Puls,
I can see her now,
urging me on.

Ashokan Farewell

—for Alie, Christmas Eve, 2007

Just now it is no more farewell
than hello, hello to the gift

unwrapping itself in sound,
my granddaughter at fifteen

handling the violin with a confidence
both delicate and precise, and

I love her for loving what she is doing,
each part of her a part of what

she is playing, farewell to Ashokan,
hello to the gift she is giving, her lips

pursed, her keen eyes following
the quick liquid flow of her fingers,

her smile, when she sees me smiling,
saying *You're welcome, old man*

with ears made of consummate tin.
You are welcome!

At Mo Java

—for Harold Hall

When I told my colleagues that recently
I spent eight days on an island
surrounded completely by water

he said that's what an island is by
definition, you dumb tourist,
and of course I knew that already, but

what I didn't know, or expect, was that
he would fail to appreciate the humor
in my remark, so to indicate my chagrin

I said *sandy beach!* instead of *son
of a bitch!*, which amused him because
he too had been raised on euphemisms

intended not to offend a god who kept
copious notes. The island surrounded
entirely by water was Oahu,

its daily sun severe enough to turn
an idler's fishbelly skin into flesh red
as a baboon's assend, proof of which

I had seen more than experienced, thanks
to sunscreen and a cautious and protective
woman. We were drinking coffee, my

colleague and I, in a small hangout
surrounded completely by others drinking
coffee. Tomorrow we'll be in our respective

homes, hibernating, snow falling and
more on the way, no two flakes alike, I'm
told, though like the traffic at Waikiki

to me they'll all look pretty much the same.

At Risky's Bar & Lounge

We sit in a booth, my colleague and I,
sipping cold beer and wondering
whether our waitress knows, or cares,
about what one of us learned this morning
about sparrow hawks. They can see
eight times more clearly than Homo sapiens.

She is lean and young and moon-faced
and clear-eyed and her cancer, she told us,
is in remission. Yes, thank you—and cheese-
burgers to complement the beer. I tried not
to stare at a growth of what looked to be fur,
young rabbit fur, that covered her head,
and I was reminded that one of the families
of marsh rabbits—*Sylvilagus palustris*
hefneri—is named after *Playboy's*
Hugh Hefner.

And that isn't all: The Kori Bustard is
perhaps the largest bird ever to have been
capable of flight—up to forty pounds and
four feet long.

She delivers the cheeseburgers with a grin,
wants to know if we'd like another beer.
Sure, we say, when you have the time.

We move from birds to an entry in my
colleague's notebook: *louche*, meaning
of questionable taste or morality. From
the French, its translation *squint-eyed*,
from the Latin *luscus*, or *blind in one eye.*

I had a friend in high school, I say,
who was blind in one eye and couldn't
see out of the other. Even now, I say,
I can picture him clearly.

She brings us the beers. We sip. We talk.
It is August. The fans overhead go around
and around. If I focus on a single blade
I can follow it for maybe a full revolution.
The clock on the east wall, with its lighted
Clydesdales prancing, tells us to drink
Budweiser. In a few years no smoking
will be permitted at Risky's, no smoking
in any public facility in the state anywhere.

But at the moment a haze hangs cirrus and
indifferent in the air. The Budweiser is cold,
delicious, immediate. If I were a sparrow
hawk I could see it eight times more clearly.
If I were a Kori Bustard I could, in spite
of the odds against me, take wing. And when
our waitress returns I'll ask her to remove
her apron and join us. I want to give her
the keys to the kingdom. O somebody, please,
attend me! I want to touch her hair.

Balance Beam

—for Nikki and Lance
upon the occasion of their marriage,
October 16, 2009, Topeka, Kansas

When my eyes aren't open they are closed,
and clearly then I see it happening—the
lapse, the wobble, the stumble, the fall,
beside me the hand of someone touching

> my hand, telling me with its feel how the
> routine is going, until I can bear it no
> longer. And I open my eyes to see a figure
> on the balance beam beautifully balanced,

balanced both in stasis and in flight, bare-
footed gymnast now airborne, now
returned to the beam to pose with her arms
extended as wings—now a turn, a leap, a flip,

> a handstand, a leg-split, balance on a beam
> of polished wood four inches wide and four
> feet high, balance when later she becomes
> the one in white to attend us, balance then as

she falls for the one who will catch and hold
her, balance in the sweet, sweet composite
of affection, balance in the steps they will
take as, down an aisle, after vows, they exit,

> balance in the rhythm the arms and hands will
> make as they wave goodbye, goodbye, all of us
> high on our toes waving back and reaching
> out, as if to hold what we cannot grasp as

beneath us the earth, four inches wide and
in dutiful balance with its countless mothers
and fathers, brothers and sisters, bodies
heavenly and otherwise, goes right on turning.

The Bear I Knew Was There

> —*I… followed unmarked paths left*
> *by stars too wild to show themselves*
> *anywhere but here, inhaled her nursing*
> *musk, the bear I knew was there.*
>
> —Peggy Shumaker, "Just This Once,"
> in *Just Breathe Normally*

was not there, but what I knew
when I looked at the place
where I knew she was

was that she had been there,
knew that she yet existed,
that because she was

not there she must be elsewhere,
that wherever she was she
knew I'd find her,

knew in her ursine bones that one
day her far-off cousin
would find her,

knew that when that day arrived
she had best be prepared,
claws sharpened,

growl at a disconcerting pitch, legs
fully conditioned, two
to rise on, two

to extend for both of us, when the
time arrives, her warmest
welcome.

Change

After the change that we know lies ahead
lies another, then another,
behind us meanwhile a wobbly contrail

of roadways and pathways festooned and
littered with changes. Why, then,
do those images in the mirror so confound

and amaze us? The hand that rises to touch
her now is the same that touched
her then, though at the least a thousand times

changed. In that new cotton blouse, blue as
the heavens, she has become
another specimen the scope of science has yet

to identify. And for the longest time we
stand not moving, our faces
posing for the photo we will one day find

where neither remembers having placed it,
and we'll look at it and smile,
and nod, and throw ourselves, at last, away.

Childhood

—for Will Locke

I have heard him say it so many times
I almost believe it: It is never too late
to have a happy childhood.

He is a strong, tall, rugged man who can
hardly wait to run the Pikes Peak
marathon again.

> How patient must we be to learn at last
> the value of patience? I have things to do,
> said the malingerer back home, grinning
> widely. Things to do, and caps on the necks
> of countless bottles to unscrew. Yet
> he seldom left the slats of the bench
> he sat on. It was his way
> of confronting with words whatever
> adventure he might otherwise
> have jumped into.

My undaunted friend, so thoroughly human,
has known many times the fickle
consequences of time and chance. But always
there is, for him, another mountain to ascend,
and so—living for a moment the childhood
he can't stop living—he ascends it.

It's the thin air at the top, he says later.
He is showing me the photos another runner
took. In this one, a close-up, his pose is all lips
and teeth. It's the thin air, he says again. It
makes you appreciate the value of that
which enables you to go on climbing.

What he wants more than anything:
a mound of earth so high it has no pathway
leading down. And how high might that
be? Only the one who arrives there
knows, and mercifully, like the hiker
whose thumb always fails,
he remains on the way.

Dialogue

—But where are you, reader,
who have not paused in your walk
to look over my shoulder
to see what I am jotting in this notebook?

—Billy Collins, "August in Paris," in *Ballistics*

I'm here in the TV room, my friend, here
in Lincoln, Nebraska, my walk finished, and I am
reading your poems as I watch the Tigers

and Twins go at it, not that I much care who wins
or loses, because I'm married to the National League,
and in case you don't know it I'll tell you, a vow

is a vow, and having kept mine for more than
half a hundred years I continue to delight
in whatever complements any one of my several

biases—the inscription I saw last week on an
infant's T-shirt, for example, infant asleep in its
daddy's large arms as the cameraman brought

the words close enough to be read: *I can't even*
walk yet, and already I hate the Yankees.
I should say, though, that your poems are

competitive. During commercials I read them, and
more times than not I'm still reading them as Curtis
Granderson, say, homers with two on

to put the game away for the Tigers, you meanwhile
explaining what a bathtub family is or how
all of us are "ensnared … in the same mortal coil,"

the Bard himself in his own day ensnared, and
certainly also Pete Reiser and Jackie Robinson
and you, my friend, and I, and everyone

in the Church of Saint Thomas Aquinas that day
you watched it being painted by a man in a flannel
shirt—and the artist himself, even though

his painting, let's say, will be deemed eventually
a masterpiece and will be sold at auction
for more money than any of us other mortal

coils, ensnared, could shake a crepuscular fist at.

Early Morning in Early October, 2009

I can't go back to sleep
because Hopkins' sprung rhythms
are bouncing in my skull like those rubber balls

I practiced with when, as
a boy, I believed in the redemptiveness
of juggling. My brother could do it, juggle I mean,

and he was two years
younger. The eyes of the girls who watched
first forgave, then adored, him. Now Margaret, one

of her rhythms so deftly
sprung, is grieving. She has been watching
the leaves fall from a golden grove, but she does not

truly understand why
such a sight should so sadden her. Hopkins
knows. But should he tell her? They forgave my

brother, the girls did,
because they must have viewed
forgiveness as a prerequisite to adoration. And

my brother, smart as
a whip, good humored and ornery, begged,
without saying a word, forgiveness. Margaret does

not want the lovely
trees to lose their leaves. No leaves, no
loveliness—only the bare branches left to confront

the winter. Difficult
it is to go back to sleep, sprung rhythms
bouncing in the skull, Margaret meanwhile, whether

or not she wants it,
receiving an unvarnished conclusion: *It is
Margaret you grieve for.* Not Margaret only, but

finally Margaret,
Margaret somehow intuiting that one day
she too, like the leaves from a *Goldengrove*, must

fall. And my brother,
his bright eyes on each rubber ball, each
orange, each apple, each egg brought fresh and

vulnerable from the
henhouse, catches each object softly, as if
an infant dropped from a great, great height, each

wholeness then
in the blink of an eye aloft and,
in the care of my brother's hand, sustained.

Early November, 2008

Leaves are falling. I have cast my vote and now, returning
home, I am pausing on the planks of a bridge
to watch the water in Antelope Creek

find its way to some distant joining. Leaves, falling: orange
into rust into the colors the sunset will assume
come evening. The woman I am with

is the woman I was with when this voyage began. Separately,
we cast our votes together. Now, our hands
on the rail at the side of the bridge,

we watch leaves falling, some of them finding the water in
Antelope Creek, each a lightness borne slowly
in the current, one from a sycamore

like a wide open hand cradling the sun. When the moment
seems right we'll move on, she ahead of me,
kicking the leaves, I admiring her pace,

the tireless movement of her legs. We have cast our votes,
both of which will be noted tonight as we sit
with books in our laps watching and

listening to the returns. Leaves meanwhile are falling, too
many to count or assimilate, orange into rust
into sunset. I'll have watched it, the

sunset, before the closing of the polls. Eloise will have
called it to my attention, whereupon
I'll join her to do the watching.

Colors like those of the leaves we saw falling, she'll say,
and I'll nod, and later, numbers
on the screen beginning

to rival those of the falling leaves, I'll remember her as she
walked ahead of me, the pace, the scissoring
of tireless legs, both of us moving

and kicking leaves—not angrily, but festively, like children
whose hopes are the rhythms they dance to
long before the music begins.

Fairbanks, Mid-July

—for Jake

Far from home, not watching my grandson
play his final game of junior-league baseball,
I look up to see a small white sphere
falling slowly, its background a blue sky
vast as all creation. Will I be able
to run under it in time to make the catch?

I enter a church to face the congregation
to share my epiphany: Centerfield
is the center of the universe.

The shackles they bind me in do nothing
to impede the movement of the white sphere
downward, nothing to arrest the progress
of my own momentum.

On the Chena River a widgeon
bobs in the current, its elegant upright body
drifting backward like royalty
downstream.

I have managed somehow to outlast
the walls of my unpadded cell. Above me,
the white sphere continues to descend. The out-
field, grass-green, is made of grass. And

what about it do I most admire? O brothers
and sisters, hear me: It has no end.

He is wearing a uniform that's mostly white,
his last name in red letters
across the upper back, cap and stockings
Dodger blue. With him I sense the sweet collapse of distance.
There is not now, or ever was, a turning back.

Feathers

In my hand
I hold the sacred feathers.

I am ready.
I hear the drumbeat, steady,

and over it the drone
of countless suns and moons.

When I grow older
I want to be more of what just now

I am.
Who in this universal tipi

owns the skins it's made of?
Who the land?

And in the name of all of us
as yet unborn

I ask: How long
must the music play

before we begin
our dancing?

Fish

Fish have no word for fire, not even
when above it they sizzle and pop
enticingly in the skillet.

It's an old one, ancient really, its
cast iron too heavy almost
for the boy who,

at the request of his mother, dragged
it into the kitchen from where
on the back porch

it had held the dirt that nourished
the petunias until it was time
to transplant them.

She had soaked and scoured the skillet
until its blackness gleamed
as the white towel

dried it, the boy meanwhile standing
bewildered and proud,
bewildered that

his mother would make such a fuss
over the fish, because
hadn't he run away

to Anthony's pond to catch it? And
hadn't he been told that if he
did it again he'd

be given the whipping of his life?
And he was proud that now
his mother in a blue

apron with a yellow chicken on it
was at the skillet, humming
something he thought he

recognized but would not remember
until he was in bed,
almost asleep,

Amazing Grace, and then the bobber
would dip and come back up
and dip again,

this time disappearing, mudcat so
belly-heavy he could
scarcely believe his

eyes, but now, the flesh of the catch
sizzling and popping
in the skillet,

cottonwood aflame in the range, he
said to himself what his
father might have

said had he been there to say it, *son
of a bitch*—not in
resentment or

anger, but as a simple validation
of thrill and dread—his
mother humming,

fire that fish have no name for
calling, in the voice of the
diminishing, to be fed.

Forecast

It's funny, but without her
laughter is the child
who has no one to play with.

I sit in my padded chair
listening for the *hush hush hush*
of her downy slippers.

When the forecast calls for rain
I move everything of value
into the attic,

where a blown-away shingle
tells me I have nothing
to fear.

Sunlight. I wish she were here
to see it. It is not enough,
of course,

it having neither substance
nor shadow, but for
the moment,

until the prediction comes
amazingly true, it
is everywhere.

Golden Years My Ass

My original intention was to write a book-length memoir
in which I'd chronicle the dwindling days
of my life, being careful

to underscore the heartaches and disillusionments,
especially those obscenely high prices
of gasoline and medications,

and noting also the greater miseries—misplacing the keys,
misplacing the car for which the mis-
placed keys were intended,

the ever-present however distant threat of incontinence.
But I am enjoying myself too much
to write a lengthy piece

with the title *Golden Years My Ass,* though it was this
title, and the myriad of misfortunes
that lurked like voyeurs

behind it, that gave me the memoir idea in the first place.
And now here I am on the patio,
drinking hot black coffee

while watching the man with his mower cut the grass,
listening to the song his machine
makes as swath after green

swath levels the lawn and, when my wife joins me, for
some unaccountable reason we begin
to sing our high school

fight song, her alto joining my baritone, the sound of
the mower joining in, two geezers
and a mower making

harmony—*We'll raise a song, both loud and long,*
to cheer our team to vic-to-ry—not
Golden Years My Ass at all,

but more like *Golden Years Are Here Again*, crackers
and rockets exploding all over the place,
confetti falling like shredded

manna from the overhead, the swell aroma of potassium
nitrate in league with the new-mown
grass—*for AHS, so brave and*

strong, we pledge e-ter-nal loy-al-ty—my wife grinning
as we sing, that same gat-toothed grin
I parked so many, many times

in the catalpa grove with, and suddenly the mower
is gone, and with it its
consonant whine,

giving our song the occasional silences it so needs
to resonate—*fight on, boys, fight,*
we'll win this game,

raise high the score for At-ti-ca—our cups in our hands
now, now raised for the toast—
beneath the fold

of black and gold, to vic-to-ry for AHS!—whereupon
we touch one cup to the other and,
no longer enfeebled, together

we drink.

Letter From A Long-Time Friend

Not finally illegible, this letter from a long-time friend,
because like the daily crossword
eventually, word by word, I solve it, my friend's dips

and doodles and looping flourishes so primly complex
I marvel at the hand that shaped them,
small hand, I know, for a man so large, so muscular,

it being nonetheless the hand, or so my friend has told
me, that in the ring could deliver
counter-punches too swiftly for most of his opponents

to see them coming, but the few exceptions, he said,
convinced him to try a different
occupation, so now he is using the hand to write with,

narratives delivered as poetry, their characters lifting
themselves from the page
to become the breath and the blood so familiar

to those whose breath and blood they share, some
of them heroic, some pitiful, some
hilarious, all of them the consequence of dips and

doodles and looping flourishes that in an earlier life
I'd have labeled sissy, and the one
who shaped them pantywaist, my own hand meanwhile

utterly maverick and therefore masculine, except that
on the playground it somehow
couldn't manage to find the jaw of the shitass most

deserving, and I'd tongue the blood on my swollen lip,
tasting the thick sweet residue
of miscalculation, on my desk then in the classroom

problems of impossibly long division, in front of me
the girl whose thick dark hair I wanted
to touch, but never did, my hand with its wooden fingers

working to find the answer that, should I ever find it,
would enable me to move into the
remainder of my improbable days to look for another.

Little Colorado

It's in my neighbor's backyard—not a mountain
with a stream gushing downward over rocks,
but a single aspen,

and just now, it being late October, its leaves
are blushing as they quake, and I think
of my buddy Gladden,

most alone in the presence of others, how we'd
take our own sweet time walking home
after school, always

Gladden's home, a small stuccoed house where
he lived with his mother and spooky aunt,
her long nose and marble eyes

appearing and disappearing suddenly, silently,
Gladden not taking note, I always
on the lookout, his Philco

meanwhile alive with the voice of Jack Armstrong
or the Lone Ranger or America's Ace
of the Airwaves, Hop

Harrigan—*CX4 to control tower, CX4 to control
tower, this is Hop Harrigan taking off*—
my buddy Gladden grinning

like a gopher, I beside him grinning also, but
aware that at any moment his
spooky aunt might

materialize, her face precisely that of Hop's
Ghostly Avenger, and there we
were, Gladden and I,

fifth-graders in league with characters and plots
our teacher, we believed, never
dreamed of, our

conversations before the opening bell, and at
recess, consisting only of bits and
pieces of dialogue

from the Philco, coded messages the others did
not understand, our secrets encoded
in smiles and nods

worthy of the most indelicate sin: *CX4 to control
tower, CX4 to control tower, this is
Hop Harrigan coming in.*

Lonesome For Hymns

As a genetic Lutheran, probably a Sunday-school
contributor to Chinese missions, and semi-retired
church musician, I was lonesome for hymns.

—Bill Holm, *Coming Home Crazy*

It's a familiar longing, Bill, a disease actually,
and curable chiefly by immersing yourself
in the cacophony of far-fetched metaphor—

... for I have opened up tow'rd heaven
all the windows of my soul,
and I'm living on the hallelujah side ...

In the pew beside you, if you're lucky, sits a wide,
comfortable woman; she is holding a hymnal
in her potato fingers, her whiskey voice

contributing mightily to the immersion you
so needed to stanch the flow of loneliness,
her passion becoming your own,

and buoyed by her outpourings you clutch the
lifeline she has thrown you, whereupon, un-
daunted, you indulge a few outpourings of your own—

... oh glory be to Jesus, let the hallelujahs roll,
help me ring the Savior's praises far and wide ...

And thinking of you sitting there, soothing lone-
liness with the unlikely balm of a far-flung Gilead,
I find myself at your other side, my own sorry bulk

desiring if not outright needing to contribute
in order to justify the melodious mayhem, my
voice with its low-down timbre aching to join in:

... for I have opened up tow'rd heaven
all the windows of my soul,
and I'm living on the hallelujah side ...

It pleases me, brother, that as a genetic Lutheran
you yielded to the wiles of dissonant temptation,
pleases me further that with words on the page

you invited me to take a seat beside you, to aid
and abet in the committing of a righteous felony,
later to be found so blessedly guilty, to be thereafter

spending our days in our mutual cells no longer
lonesome, but together, somehow,
and fulfilled.

Loves

a 44-year-old man was arrested yesterday
on Safeway's parking lot having simulated
sex with his car. His pants had fallen
to his ankles.

—news item

My first was a 1938 all-black four-door Chevy,
its knob on the steering wheel enabling me
to cut a kitty on a dime,

my love for it enhanced not only by its obedience
but likewise its intimate interior,
padded and unstained

until a different love became the love I'd use the
first one to make love in intervened,
static on the radio

I loved giving way to words I loved—*They tried*
to tell us we're too young—her head
on my shoulder

as, under moon and stars, headlights doused, we'd
crawl in low gear along the north side
of the windbreak,

and There's Orion, I'd say, and she'd reach herself
across me to see where I was pointing,
and more often than not

she'd say she saw it also, Orion the Hunter, she'd
say, as if saying it helped her see it,
and because the music

I loved had given way to static, I'd hush the radio
and offer my own rendition, *too*
young to really be

in love, alto from the throat of the one I loved
joining in, and there we were,
Chevy and its driver

and its driver's girlfriend, trinity moving slowly
toward where the stars were
leading, a secret place

at the center of the windbreak (mostly pines),
where the effluvia of needles
and passion remained

long after the remarkable era had ended, long
after the truth of the moment
passed (Chevy

with the cover of its domelight newly cracked):
we were not too young
at all.

Malaise

I confront my perennial malaise
by tap-dancing on the kitchen table,
which is large and oak and perfectly round,

it having been purchased at a great
price, or so my maternal grandmother
told me, purchased from the only furniture

store in town, R. O. Williamson,
proprietor, R. O. slim and stately with
a mustache to match, my feet now assuming

lives of their own, my neocortex
jingling at irregular intervals, and I
apologize, Grandmother, for not having

removed the salt & pepper shakers
before the cure began, but heaven knows
I can't stop now, salt & pepper in the dancing

no less than in the shakers, each
of which has been sent flying by feet
gone berzerk, oxfords clicking and snapping

as if weapons chattering on a
main line of resistance, tracers and
crossfire so impressive the enemy goes

to its knees, maybe to wave
the white flag of surrender, maybe
not, in which case I'll turn to a tactic

handed down from the woman
who passed down the table I'm just now
about to relinquish—onion bits simmered

in syrup, one teaspoon, two
teaspoons, three teaspoons, four,
my consolation being this: If the malaise

doesn't kill me, the onion
syrup will, whereupon I'll slow-
dance into that great ballroom in the sky,

its air cool and as pure as
the partner who nursed me and
nurses me yet back to the land of the living.

Miss Yoder

What our fifth-grade teacher did not read
to us was the story the next day we
could not remember. Instead,

she read the story that day into day
became the poem we could not
forget—though just now

I cannot remember the name of the
heroine or the color of her eyes,
or the cut of the shirt worn

by the hero who eventually might rescue
her. I remember the mouth
of my teacher, the full lips

and the white teeth, the corrugations that
were her face, and the sound
that came from the quiver

in her lovely throat. Her name, Miss Yoder.
Her thick hair wound in a bun. Her
affection for the words

she was reading. I remember that I loved
her, love her yet, remember that
I was sure my buddy Gladden

loved her too, though he was thin and shy
and therefore never said so. Her
standing so tall, so stately

before us, all of us lost in the wilderness
of her character and plot and point
of view, all of us—

having eaten the map we were told to guard
with our very lives—wanting never
to find the way.

A Moment of Delicate Balance

—for Tracy Ann, July 10, 2009

In the palm of my right hand
I hold my infant daughter
as if a trophy I somehow
deserve. Note the fullness
of the child's eyes, their innocence,

their amazement. Note also
the position of the father's free hand,
how ready it is to save the day.
And the father's mouth: half open,
and tentative, it speaks—how shall I

say it?—volumes. What you cannot
see is the child's mother standing
outside the frame,
wringing her hands,
telling the father good Lord

to be careful, to lower the child
to safety, that enough is enough, let's
stop this foolishness this instant.
And soon enough that will happen.
But for the moment there is the moment,

the delicate balance, daughter and father
suspended, time unable to change
what it brought to pass—the giddiness
of joy, the unrequited height
of deep affection.

My Father, Whistling

Not an easy tune to whistle, "The Great
Speckled Bird," but he did it, my father, I believe
because he thought there was no one around,

I being almost always no one, and just
as frequently not around. I'd come upon him, say,
as he lay under the family Ford, about

to loosen the threaded bolt to release the
spent oil to make room for the fresh. Sunday, say,
a warm afternoon in April, Sunday school,

with its story of Moses lying safely
in the arms of the bullrushes, left suspended high
and dry on a flannelboard, the sweet lofty

notes of my father's whistling escaping
from the maw of an upraised hood, notes I had
no choice but to put the words to: *What a*

beautiful thought I am thinking, concerning
a great speckled bird. I thought more than spoke
the words, amazed beyond belief that

my father and I could do such a thing
together, and do it so precisely, so delicately
on key, perhaps because we could not

see each other, making each of us some-
how elsewhere: *Remember her name is recorded
on the pages of God's Holy Word.* Until

of course the threaded plug would refuse
to yield, and the speckled bird gave way to curses
less lofty but equally melodious,

God being told to damn the son-of-a-bitching
bolt all to hell, my father's legs, what I
could see of them, rising and falling like

pistons in their overalls, his voice
escaping harsh and intense from the maw of the
upraised hood, a clattering of wrench

against bolt ominous as the morning
sermon, Gog and Magog let loose upon the grip
of one God-damned because unrelenting

threaded bolt, grunt and gasp and knuckles
I'll notice later bleeding, myself silent as the salt
Lot's wife was turned to, cadence and rhythm

of my father's voice so beautifully
delivered, until hallelujah wrench and flesh
prevail, and I can hear oil falling into itself

in the blue enameled pan discarded by
my mother, oil falling into itself the only sound—
until the last of the oil drips into the pan, and

what's out of sight is what I envision most
clearly—my father's fingers, steady, deliberate,
replacing the bolt, lips pursed as if ready

to whistle whatever the moment calls for—
ready because he has won, ready because though
I'm nearby I'm nowhere, nobody, to be seen.

My Understanding

One of many, it came not so much in the plot of the story
delivered by the lips and the throat and the tongue
of my Sunday school teacher, Mrs. Heath,

who spoke of one special sheep that wandered far away
from the herd, a *stray* she called it, how when
it was discovered missing its shepherd

left his flock to search for it—and mind you, she said, he
did not relinquish the search until he had found
it, whereupon he cradled it in his arms

and returned it to the fold—as it was in the sound of the
old woman's voice, its intonations, so soft, so
reassuring, its rhythms rising and falling,

its words at times so delicate and absolute. Ah, *fold.* Ah,
stray and *flock, mind you* and *relinquish* and
cradled, each a sheep in its own way

being found and delivered, and this is my understanding,
no more the saving of the sheep than
the measured delivering of words

that brought the story to me, breath from the lungs
of an old woman staying with me, my shoes
at the time, such as they were,

unable to reach the floor, the oak bench kneading my
young boy's tender rump to mush—
or later, to salt, as

with Lot's wife I turned my head to look at my buddy
Galen, both of us older now, and wiser, both
on our way to waiting for our teacher's

version of the story to work its wonders and some-
how bingo! return us to where and to what,
once upon a time, we were.

Nightfall

When we close the windows
and lower the blinds
we deny the windowpeeker, say

no to the moonslant that has risen
to lave us. Not that
we should never close the windows

and lower the blinds, our business
being our own,
not that privacy isn't

finally a private matter. But tonight
there is nothing but darkness
to do the peeking, no moon to reach us

with its thick long tongue. So who
do we think we are, anyway?
Let's toss habit to the four winds and

give the long shots their chance. Here
we are, buckaroos, let's
say. Have at it. No matter your

intentions, good or ill, tonight we are
what we are. Together. Alone.
Three stories up.

Impervious.

Night of the Half Moon

As if to compensate for what is hidden,
the visible half of the moon has doubled its
brightness, or so it seems to one who for so
many years wanted to believe in the doctrine

of natural compensation, my brother
at a tender age yielding himself to a majority
of the seven deadly sins, so to compensate
I overbrushed my teeth and scoured my flesh

with Lifebuoy and gave my heart to Jesus
on a bi-weekly basis. I stand now
at the largest window in a house
that is blessedly small, watching a moon

so perfectly halved I cannot be sure
whether it's waxing or waning: It loves
me, it loves me not. Tomorrow at this time
I'll know, unless clouds obscure the answer,

in which case I'll make an informed guess
or wait for the skies to clear, patience being
an acknowledged, if not one
of the seven cardinal, virtues. My brother

meanwhile, having lifted himself by his boot-
straps, has lifted me by bringing me mercifully
down, his dark side serving to compensate
for my ungodly, because unnatural, sheen—as if

my life were not a full moon because only
one half was showing, as if to deny is to
remove the dust that stops uncountable
mouths, as if only the visible can be seen.

No Open Casket

You don't want to see him, he said,
and my brother and I didn't argue, not because
we regarded the mortician as someone

too imperial to be confronted, but because
several days ago we had seen the brown paper sack
containing our father's blood-drenched

effects—jeans, plaid shirt, socks, under-
clothes, billfold—belongings handed to us by the
officer who described what must have

happened. And, too, the old Dodge, its
brown crumpled body a testimony to the power
of impact. No, we said, we don't, and

we didn't, and the stranger who presided (un-
like the Baptist dervish who seasons earlier
at the gravesite of our father's meek

second wife spoke more than he knew,
much more, until finally, chilled to the bone
by pretention and a brisk north wind,

I whispered to my brother, *Let's attack
and dismember the sorry bastard; I'll make a
cradle of my arms to carry off the parts*, but

my brother, though more often than not
reasonable, shook his head, and the dervish alas
survived) spoke slowly and softly, saying

chiefly what we had told him, that the one we
did not want to see was neither more nor less than
what he was, a decent husband and father,

and the place prepared for him seemed
to agree, seemed willing to swap its emptiness
for something to fill it, sight unseen.

No Substitute

*And though sometimes you couldn't see the person
  you were with,
there was no substitute for that person.*

—Louise Gluck, "Midsummer"

No substitute, because what made the person
forever special
was an absence of eyes to gaze into,

a depletion of blush on the cheekbone, cheek-
bone less to be
seen than touched, the pitch-black night an exercise

in Blindness 101, golly Moses and sakes alive,
and one step
becomes the mile you'll say you traveled

when the sun rises and you see clearly how
murky clarity
can be, another evening meanwhile on its way

to inviting you into its warmly unfamiliar grotto,
its movement
painfully, divinely slow, its eventual darkening

closing the eyes you nonetheless keep open
as the one
for whom there is no substitute joins you

in your quest to do whatever must be done
to make the
moment, beyond the moment, immeasurable.

Not Caring

When finally I told her
how much I loved her
she told me she couldn't care less.

I was not yet independently wealthy,
but the 1938 Chevy was free of scars—
and paid for.

Think of it, I said,
as a dowry. Agiggle, she told me
she couldn't care less.

Hindsight tells me this:
I was ready to settle down, but
she wanted only what she labeled *fun*.

And for the brief duration of summer
it was. Not even the gear stick
could come between us.

But the summer ended, and where
she wandered, and
how far, is anybody's guess.

Now on Saturday nights
I drive the Chevy from the tracks
at the south side of town

to the high school at the other, slowly,
windows down, country
on the radio, with each song

static crisp as bacon in a cast-iron skillet
holding up its end
of an endless conversation.

Not the Same Reader Twice

There are so many stories,
more beautiful than answers.

—Mary Oliver, "Snake"

Because I am never the same reader twice
I return to the lines that earlier
had sent me to the garage to attempt
something ornamental.

The project required first the drilling
of a small hole into a chunk of rock, then
the fitting of a slender steel rod
into the hole. Metamorphic, the rock.

When I first read the lines I was struck
by their simplicity, so many others
having said the same weary thing. I know, I
know. Death isn't easy.

I used a masonry bit, but the first one broke.
The next one finally did the job, but barely. I
had cursed like a fiend. My father, such a long
time gone, would have grinned.

The lines are in a poem I'd rather not share.
But all right, here's the ending: *Life*
must go on. I forget just why. It's a brief
poem—twenty-two short lines, to be exact.

Then I smoothed a short length of bur oak to
assume the shape of a cattail. Smooth
as a bean, this lovely finger of oak. So
gratifying to the touch, so freshly aromatic.

The mother in the poem is speaking to her
children, telling them their father is dead. Saying
she will make them jackets and small trousers
from his old coats and pants, telling them ....

With a wood bit I drilled a hole into the length
of bur oak, eased the rod then into the hole. It's
amazing, isn't it, how this and that
can sometimes fit together?

From the pockets of the father's pants the mother
will remove pennies and keys, the former
to be saved in the son's bank, the latter
for the daughter to make a *pretty noise* with.

On the mantle between two photos of the most
recent grandchildren the cattail, on its slender
metal stalk, tremors. And this: *Anne, eat
your breakfast. Dan, take your medicine.*

I have read that, thanks to its bark, the bur oak
can survive the fiercest prairie fire. Yet
I wonder. I go to where I believe I read it first
to read it again.

Only Yesterday

Because my body is suffering
from an insufficiency of vitamin D
I am sitting with pad and pencil

in the sunshine in a chair made
of blue plastic strips and aluminum.
It was my wife who delivered

the diagnosis, vitamin D being
at the moment her specialty. And to
tell you the truth, the treatment

isn't especially painful. True, the
mid-afternoon sun squints the eyes,
but without it the golden leaves

on the trees would not be as golden,
and the euonymus would not be ablaze.
It was the bush, wasn't it, that Moses

with his own deficiencies saw in
the desert, burning. Golly, Moses, I
remember when you were a baby

lying hushed and endangered
in the bullrushes. It seems like only
yesterday. To tell you the truth,

I feel better already. True, the
impatiens have folded, but their going
has brightened the yellow on the

mums, a cluster of which my
nurse will tease into a centerpiece
for the kitchen table, which is

oak and perfectly round and, at
a place and time far removed from this
aluminum chair, belonged to my

fallen mother's long-departed mother.

Playing the Favorites

—for Willie

I watch the horses
on-screen from Sarasota,
that graveyard of favorites,
but I can't desist: I too play
chiefly the favorites—Armstrong Mill,
Powerful Appeal, Hastobegood, Wild Bishop,
Angry Hombre, Seattle Shine.

And my grandson also,
Wilhelm in German, Will To Win
in translation, how, after the broken jaw,
the busted chin, teeth scattered
in each of the four great directions,
he rallies at the far turn and, as

I watch the horses
on-screen at Sarasota,
I can't desist: I play again the favorites—Step
Lively, Pepper Jazz, Summer Hero, Shot Blocker,
Write It Down and, at the near turn,
leading the pack, that outside
entry: Wilhelm in German,
in translation Will To Win.

Pursuing the Friendship of Water

*... the body unlearning its weight as it plunged to the black
of the deep end and came, at a stroke,
to the friendship of water.*

—John Burnside, "Learning to Swim"

It's a long race that has no final line
short of nihility,

but you run it anyway, afraid you'll one day
cross the line that isn't there,

your body in a body of water
less terrified than relieved, water, sure

enough, the best lover, touching you
at once all over,

friendship in the mirror you're in
confirming friendship,

your arms, your legs eager to take you
to the deepest hole

in the pool, to bring you up when you're
down,

to deliver you cleansed and refreshed and
breathing

to the shallows where not even night
seems a menace,

and the death that existed only
in forethought is gone.

Reflection

The creek is better than I am
at accepting my aging face.

—Edward Harkness, "Rattlesnake Creek, South Fork"

Not so the mirror I stood in front of
this morning, not a funhouse mirror, certainly,
but an honest one,

so much so, in fact, that I called for
my wife to serve as a witness to our mirror's
efficacy.

In her blue chenille bathrobe she stood
beside me, told me that, yes, our mirror does
indeed know

its onions, which surprised me—not
her complicity, but her use of a metaphor with
onions in it,

her nose upturned at their slightest
effluvium. So I swallowed what little was left
of my pride

and nodded. What I didn't say is
what I'll say just now, and one time only—that
 I'd like to spend

the rest of my hours and days
in a country where streams are as common as
the pebbles they flow over, my face

on the unspeckled surface ageless
and scoured and, in the midst of such tireless
movement, not moving.

Rhapsody for a Lingering Weekend in Brighton, Colorado

—in memory of Mary Ann

Slowly the late afternoon light is fading, its only
option. Night, then, has no choice
but to follow.

>And I remember how once upon a time,
>in a vastness of conifers,
>we maneuvered a pathway that, before we
>appeared on the scene, was neither path
>nor way. Pyramids of pine cones.
>Haystacks of needles. And
>not far away a medley
>of aspens, quaking.

In the kitchen the aroma of lasagna
loosens our tongues. For a moment we are
reflective, joyous, undaunted, profound—
filled to the brim with the milk
of human cohesion.

>Should my brother John be apprehended?
>He is practicing medicine without a license,
>abetting a catheter to drain fluids
>from his wife's shunted lungs. And
>though just now she is alert and dutifully
>cheerful, we know what we know—
>she is late afternoon light, fading.

At the races that distant day we scorned the odds,
bet the farm on the number seven horse
in the seventh race. I don't believe
in superstitions, said my brother. It's

bad luck. Maybe. But son of a bitch, would
you believe it? Number seven won.

     Rocks, rocks, rocks, each with a voice
     of its own. That one repeating *hold me* is
     the one I'll pocket. I will take it with me—
     where?

     Everywhere.

If I could sing I'd sing the song I'd write—
if I could write one. What the rock says is what
I hear: *I am what I am, and where.*

     Not so far away the mountains rise
     to define the ups and the downs of a skyline.
     Even when I can feel its presence, the rock
     is more there than here. Remembering this,
     I find it a consolation.

Approaching night smells like leaves
just recently rained on.
They haven't yet fallen, at least not
most of them, but give them
what they'll receive—eventually.
Give them time.

     Laughter from the throat of the one
     whose fluids hang in a delicate balance. Laughter
     from the throats of those beside her. If I could
     sing I'd sing the song I'd write—
     if I could write one.

Now the light, because it is finished, can begin
to reassert itself once more. And night,
its choices always and forever down to one,
begins again to shine.

Saturday, Early April

He is among us:--as in times before!
And we who toss and lie awake for long,
Breathe deep, and start, to see him pass the door.

—Vachel Lindsay, "Abraham Lincoln Walks at Midnight"

Not only at midnight, but also at mid-morning, lilacs
at the edge of blooming, scent of another day
thick with promise,

and at the homestead here in the heart of cornland
I sit on the back porch with my wife of so
many seasons. We are

cozy in chairs that murmur slightly as they rock, and
we are drinking black coffee from white
porcelain cups

passed on to us from parents, those pioneers whose
forebears were likewise pioneers, and
with the advent

of a new sun rising we listen to what a small breeze
through the limbs of a nearby oak
is whispering:

As I would not be a slave, so I would not be a master,
each syllable from our rockers joining
in. I take that to mean,

intones the woman beside me, that if I want a second
cup of coffee I must fetch it for myself.
I nod. She is gone,

and when she returns I smile, because she has brought
me a second cup also, and we
return to our watching

and listening and rocking, each chair moving at its
own independent pace, yet each a part
of what maybe it means

to have formed, to be forming yet, and then no doubt
to form, again and again and again,
a more perfect union.

Sacrament

One more bite, I told my companions, and
I'll burst, and they nodded because
I believe they too were

only one bite away from self-destruction,
burritos and beans, rice and
enchiladas and tacos

enough for a regiment. Yet not much later,
when my wife serves me
cold milk and home-

baked cookies, I drink the one and eat the
others slowly and appreciatively, as if
indulging a sacrament,

because it *is* a sacrament, and no one is
ever too sated not to have room
for a blessing, nourishment

less a concern than a fulfillment, and I am
ready now for the night—O let it
happen, all you thumpers and

pimps and orders and primates and synods
and ritualistic bimbos—
bring it on!

Sitting With My Lady Friend
at a Concert in Santa Fe, New Mexico

—for Cheryl and Ace

On a stage not far in front of us
someone with a voice smooth as a cowlick
sings something we don't recognize,

her presence a form of art
whose beauty is its brevity, unlike so many
other forms we spent the day admiring,

wood and glass and bronze
and so forth, each intended to amaze and
teach and console and soothe

and outlast us, especially the
one we almost traded the ranch for, such
tenderness in the eyes

of the woman with the thick
white hair who so reminded us of our
maternal grandmothers, and

what I want to say is that
in the midst of art our selves are the art
we look for—to amaze and teach

and console and soothe and
outlast us, our forms in pastels, say, or
sepia, forms sitting closely

together and looking to see
what those who view us can only imagine:
someone on a stage not far

in front of us with a voice
smooth as a cowlick singing something
we ancients do not recognize,

except to know that its
unerring timbre is what gives our faces the
awe the viewers will be

drawn to, their eyes, like ours,
growing dimmer by the minute, eyes, like
ours, so far from the pastures

of home, so ageless, so perfectly human.

Sitting in the Peanut Gallery in Paradise

No harps, no choirs, no avenues or boulevards
paved with gold. Mostly an infield
and an outfield and four bases that shape a diamond

much smaller than the Ritz. It's in California, of course,
state of the Angels, but the band below me
has yet to ascend to the lowest level, each a ragtag

who nonetheless knows so indelicately how to scratch
and spit. Oh it's the not-knowing
and the knowing that bring me here, the next strike

or ball neither this nor that until the divinity in blue
calls it, the certainty meanwhile of a full
moon say in the last two innings, Moon of the Home Run,

rising, and sitting alone in a crowd in the peanut gallery
in Paradise I move ever deeper into a fresh
sack of peanuts, drink deeply from a vessel that, if I plan

far enough ahead, must not, until finished, run dry.

Sitting Next to a Young Woman
Who Plays Classical Violin

Because in my childhood I learned the art of pilfering
I continue to nurture it, this time
to take from the young woman beside me
something to help me live my life
more musically, something that
by way of a quaint osmosis
will enable me to fall from the high notes
without shattering the delicate counterpoints
of flesh and bone.

She is likewise a virtuoso of slenderness,
of eyes and teeth and brow and skin
and so on. With them,
and with the kindred spirit of wood and string,
she played a spritely Hungarian piece
for all of us, its notes a lattice of tips
at the ends of fingers,
lingering.

I sit. I linger. I hear not only the sounds so recently
so generously dispensed, but also the music
of other spheres, my mother
singing so beautifully off-key
in her nocturnal effort to ease my
hell-hot fever: *Further along, we'll know all about it.*
Further along, we'll understand why. And
the spirit of wood and of string
so precisely on-key joining in, eye and teeth,
brow and skin and so on, restoration
in the presence of what, each time we recover,
can never be fully explained.

Snowbound

You're in the middle of America, snowbound,
little to do but count the flakes as they fall,
name them, watch them

gather and grow until they become the diorama
you stand at the window to study—until
from somewhere a humming

turns you, and you see her there in the kitchen
swaying, with an index finger beckoning,
and you can't resist, and

though neither of you knows how to dance
you dance—slowly, of course, but
together, she continuing

to hum, you trying to think of the name of the tune,
stew in a pot on the stove beginning to simmer,
its sound no less than its thick aroma

joining in, and there you are, an old coot with
another old coot snowbound smack
in the middle of America, warm

and confined and in spite of your prodigal feet
dancing, in your memory an image
of flake upon flake covering bile

and grime and hearts forever broken, wars and
their rumors buried deep in the silence
of whiteness, promise of seeds

buried with them bursting into bloom—not today,
not tonight, but tomorrow, sweetheart,
tomorrow—just you wait and see.

Song in Praise of the Beginning

Upon the occasion of the inauguration
of Barack Obama as the forty-fourth president
of the United States, Tuesday, January 20, 2009

Now the moment, having arrived on the backs
of so many others, extends its tireless arms
to receive the masses—the thick and the thin,

the up and the down, the dark and the light and
everyone else in between, and slow as molasses
moving in January's calm icy air

moves the moment, hope in the human breast
eternally springing, names on the parchment of time
so slowly unscrolling—those short and those tall,

the brash and the coy, the young and the weathered and
everyone else in between, and somewhere in some
grotto of memory the clickety-clack of an ancient age

yet resounding: *Now is the time for all beating hearts*
to come to the aid of their country—the near and
the far, the pumped and the weary, the believer

and otherwise and everyone else in between, and
the moment hangs on, and words joined to words
become the sentences we say with our silence

we are ready to serve—the in and the out, the halt
and the lame, the have and the not and everyone else
in between, and the grand mosaic, *as one*, sways

ever so slightly, now this way, now that, massive,
undaunted, each of its tiles interlocking, each
no more the riddle than the glory of a world

wild in its carnage to live free—the sated and the
empty, the sighted, the eyeless, the clothed
and the naked and everyone else

in between, and though there is finally a
benediction, there is no end, there is only, as
always, and for which we are grateful, the beginning.

Sounds

The sounds of passing cars
are like the sounds children make
of the sounds of cars.

—Jo McDougall, "Farm Wife"

The boy with thick lips
does the best airplane,
his brother Gene
at that moment least guarded
giving each of us a seizure
with his shrill rendition
of a housecat suddenly ignited.

The hare in its extremity,
wrote H. D. Thoreau,
cries like a child.

When I was too young
to carry a weapon
I killed my buddy
with a long whistle that ended
with a full-throated
baritone explosion.

Now something, or someone,
is making a sound
like a helicopter
delivering a dying man to the ER
of a silent hospital.

Why all at once
do I hit the deck? Because
the boy with thick lips
is coming in.

Studying for Finals

If we didn't already have feces, she said,
we'd have to invent it, and
her friend Roy did not respond because

he knew that as a history major his friend
probably was quoting someone
he didn't know, he being into psychology,

though if things didn't improve, and soon,
he was seriously considering
switching his major to something else—

animal husbandry, maybe, because he had
grown up on a farm and really
that's where his deepest roots were, though

religion wasn't out of the question, he had
roots there also, and just now,
sitting as they were in the cafeteria, studying

for finals, a few cold fries left between them,
he found himself unable
to forget what his friend had said, wondering

if the assertion was true, and, if not, then—or
so he reasoned—it must be
in its falseness a type of feces, wondering

if old Descartes had such a concept in mind
when he declared,
Je pense, donc je suis, his (the student's) ten

credit hours of French not entirely wasted,
so maybe he should
switch to foreign languages, German, say,

to augment his French, learn to say *feces*
in both German and French,
and if that failed there would always be

religion, there being always, in religion, ways
of adjusting everything,
God on his throne of purest porcelain about

to deliver from himself that which after
considerable thought
he'll elect to create, delivery then affording

a sense of pleasure he could define only
as heavenly, all of us
thereafter created in His image—or, if not

so created, given the wherewithal to invent
it, to feel our divinity then
as we study for finals or decide at last

upon animal husbandry as we milk the cows
and slop the hogs and
clean out the henhouse and change our clothes

for what in this day and age is considered dinner.

Sunday Morning on the Patio

No bells or whistles, no
hosannas in the highest, no body
nailed up and bleeding,

just the first robin of the season
posing dark-eyed and orange-breasted
on the rim of the empty birdbath,

beneath it a familiar resurrection
of green, and because suddenly
I have this odd urge

to use love, the word, in a sentence,
I tell my wife, who's sunning
nearby in a recliner, that

I love her, and when she looks up
I confuse her eyes with the
robin's, my confusion doubled

when she takes wing and glides
into the kitchen from where
very shortly she returns,

pot of coffee in one hand, cookies
in the other, her feathers molted
to reveal the skin I touched

last night before I went to sleep,
the house dark and silent,
the windows up

to admit a flow of air so steady
I let down my guard to ride
on a thermal of softness

forever, nonetheless certain that
when I alight I'll be, if not
here, then elsewhere.

Sundown Syndrome

Sundown, and the world shrinks
to become the world you lie in,

syndrome doing its best to say
you are not alone.

You are alone. The lovely woman
in white

thanks you for the samples of blood
she has taken. You say—and

you say it sincerely—You're
welcome.

Nearby, the one you have spent
the bulk of your life with

stands ready to stand where she is
indefinitely. Above,

fluorescents do their best to replicate
the sun. What your mind tells them

is that you know their devious
little game, that

you didn't just recently fall
off the turnip wagon.

You know what you know.
You are alone

a member of a group of signs and
symptoms

with a distinct connection to the sun
as it goes down. And down.

And something familiar touches
your upper arm.

Alone, you touch with the tips
of your fingers

that which is touching you. You
are alone and not

alone. Someone has parted
the curtains. Sundown.

Sundown syndrome. You
return the touch. You

watch the part in the curtains
grow darker. And

darker. Someone's
in the kitchen with Dinah.

Now it is you and the one
nearby and the one

in the kitchen with Dinah.
And Dinah. And

the one with her is strumming
on the old banjo.

Inexorably is the adverb
you think of, you

absolutely love. Because
that is the way the world is

turning. Inexorably, and
always, as the song

you relish to remember says,
toward the morning.

And Then Some

… the sound no sound makes.

—Marjorie Buettner, "Three Sijo"

It is of course the dissonance
of thought, cogs of the mind
sadly in need of lubrication.

It is most certainly the echo,
ongoing, of what they said
before the sound of no sound began.

It is surely a pity and a shame
to have let loose the hounds
of what cannot be restrained.

It is no doubt what they deserve,
they being mouths with bodies
so dutifully appended.

The good news is that bad news
rarely lasts forever.
The good news is that which

unaccountably breaks the sound
of the absence of sound, and
they are at it again,

saying all there is to say, its
sincerity unparalleled,
and then some.

Waiting

*Sometimes even a blind squirrel
finds an acorn.*

—Kansas lore

At high noon speckles of sunlight
somehow find their way through the leaves
on the oak and the horse chestnut
to heighten the green that already was green
beneath them.

I sit alone on our small patio in a metal chair
that rocks when I choose
to rock it. Now I have more than enough light
to write by.

I write that it is of considerable interest
how sunlight can so transform
something green into something greener.

I write that with its front paws a squirrel
reaches into the grass and brings forth
an acorn. When I put down my pencil
and applaud, the squirrel
cocks its head, drops the acorn,
disappears in the branches of the oak.

I pick up the pencil to further record
the behavior of the squirrel.

Because I choose to rock it, the metal chair
rocks.

I write that the metal chair rocks.

I am waiting for the sun to drop
below the lowest leaves on the horse chestnut.
When it does, I will write about
whatever it is the fallen sun reveals.

I meanwhile wait. I write that meanwhile
I wait.

Walking Ahead

They'll walk ahead, they tell us, and
my brother and I don't argue—we
know the drill, and love it:

our wives, two peas in a pod, walking
ahead, husbands behind them
surely and steadily

losing ground, until behold the women
are out of sight, but not before
the men have studied their

receding figures, backsides in a jiggling
syncopation—bear cubs wrestling
in gunny sacks, the one

beside me says, and I nod. And now, the
bear cubs having disappeared,
we pause on a small bridge

spanning a branch of the Republican.
Early October, early afternoon,
autumn flaunting itself

one hundred thousand falling leaves
at a time. Overhead, blueness
accented by white clouds

billowing. We lean on the wooden
rail to study the clear running
water: beneath it,

pebbles too many to count, glistening.
No aches, no requests, no
complaints. And

no one else to be seen. We therefore
unzip and relieve ourselves
into the river. Oh,

it's a perfect day to be doing what we
are doing, minnows at school
in the clear running

water, bird noises from a grandstand
of branches above us cheering
us on. And the girls?

Lost somewhere in this wilderness,
we say, and no doubt walking
tirelessly in circles—bear

cubs in gunny sacks, wrestling. So
when the time is ripe, and the
spoils of separation

have been sweetly and equally
depleted, we will leave
this Elysium where

we have found relief and, by the power
derived from concern,
we will join them.

Part II

David Lee

for Rob and Cheri VanWagoner
con abrazos y amor

False Alert

R. B. McCravey said
How could they tell? when Ollie McDougald
called that morning to say
It was a rumor going round
Wesley Stevens got struct and killed
by a lightningbolt during the ghost storm

Tell what? said Ollie
R. B. said If he was alive or dead
Wesley Stevens was the second sorriest
excuse for a human being he ever known of
why would anybody care?
Ollie said he didn't know
he'd try and find out

called back in an hour
said It was all false alarms
we shouldn't of got up any hopes over
R. B. said What was it then?
Ollie said Wesley Stevens' wife called
Sheriff Red Floyd said
He's outside on the ground
after the stormcloud passed over
she was purdy sure he might be
dead as one of his starved pigs
laying in the sunshine
would he come see?
Sheriff Floyd said he'd get to it directly
he knew much as anybody
Wesley wasn't much of a count
didn't have any personal interest in it
sent Deputy Sheriff Junior Shepherd
as his official representative to take charge
of the crime scene if it was any necessary

Junior Shepherd said when he got there
Wesley was kindly laying on his side
like so the sun wouldn't directly get in his eyes
with a ruler in his hand
he could have been measuring something
Junior Shepherd said Wesley are you dead any?
Wesley said Not that I know of
never even raised up or turned his head
scared Junior Shepherd two steps back
who truly didn't know yet for sure
said What you doing then
laying down on the grount like that?

Wesley said Best I can figure
we got five inches rain out that cloud
what'd yall get your side of town?
We didn't get a damn nothing Junior Shepherd said
yall got five inches
I don't see no run off I can speak of?
Look here said Wesley at these rain dents
ever one ezactly five inches
apart from the next one to it
Junior Shepherd leant over said I be damn
because for once in his life
what Wesley Stevens said was the gods' truth
Junior Shepherd put it in his report
to Sheriff Floyd and Sheila Morris the dispatcher
to be sent out to the public at large

R. B. McCravey said Well
that's one hundred percent
what I could have expected
to come out of that man's mouth
through his five inch apart mind warps
wasn't no way he was going to spend any time
in repentance over what he'd wished for
concerning either Wesley Stevens
or the need for a little rain

and how ticked off he was it didn't come again
it was all a dead false issue
under another clear blue sky
one way or another
with not a single next cloud on the horizon
nothing to celebrate or look forward to
as far as he could see

One Reason Why You Didn't Want Kristine Thornton to Talk During Town Board Meetings

while arguing over redistricting
with Joe Bob Trammel

If the Lord wanted you
to have an empty head
and a cob up your ass
He'd of put popcorn seeds
in your daddy's spurem

From sidebar minutes of the monthly
Town Board Meetings
19 September 1950

A Veritable Tale of a Wife, a Porch and a Dog

Mutt Landry said he thought
he was on the worst luckrun
of his whole live life history
didn't seem like anything
wanted to go right
drought got the first half
of the crop season
cotton didn't half come up
milo stunted as a pot-bellied dwarf pig herd
both kids grown up
moved out on him
never dreamed that would hurt
the way it plagued him
boy took the old pickup
not a day went by
he didn't need it one way or another
when the rain did come
bolls were opening
ruined almost all the rest
of the cotton and milo lodged
in the high winds
where you couldn't of even
swathed and baled it

then his wife DeeAun hired Goose Landrum
to come put a sitting porch
on the back of the house
worked maybe a week
talked her into giving him a check
for what he'd done so far
that was the last they saw of him
called and called and called
to get him to come finish the job
he'd say Oh I was just thinking

about that and meaning to come out
but I got all this work
I have to get done on a deadline
I'll get there soon's I can
finally on a Saturday morning
after DeeAun even bawled about it
Mutt called him on the telephone said
Goose by god if you don't
come finish this job of work
on my wife's porch I am
going to kill my dog
I want you to know that's a promise

DeeAun heard him say that
told him No you are not
going to kill Billy Joe
that's my final word
I need him on the front porch
as a watchdog to help me
know when the mail is come
don't you even think about that
he said to her he was so depressed
tired of fighting it out
over every single thing
from the weather to Jimmy Jack
then the pickup to the weeds
to Jenadee never calling home
to check in say she's doing okay
and the crops and now damn Goose Landrum
over that damn sitting porch he never
wanted in the first place
reminded her he already told her
Don't never ever pay
a carpenter or a plumber
till the work is all done and through
he's thinking about going down
to Bill Edwards Hardware and buy
a pistol with one bullet

get it over with for good
she said You better buy two
in case the first one don't go straight

and the phone rang
Goose Landrum saying
he would come out with a hired hand
that afternoon and get that job finished
don't go hurting that dog any
he couldn't live with the thought
of that over his head
Mutt said I'll be damned and go to hell
maybe the luck's going to change
DeeAun said Does that mean
you're not going to buy no pistol after all?
Mutt said Looks like not this year
she said Oh well then
she was hoping he'd bring back
some laundry soap and groceries
on the way back from the store
she supposed if they tried
they could find something else
to especially look forward to
if he would just cheer up a little

What Harold Rushing Told the Preacher
after the Sunday sermon
during the dust bowl drought

Reverend
I had a friend once
who studied to be a priest
in the non-true faith
and when I ast him
why he give it up
said he had to finally
tell the Lord
abstinence, poverty and chastity
aren't any one ezactly
all they cracked up to be

Odus Millard

His wife said
There was never a room
or a house where you could say
he lived in it
as much as he infested it
until he built the tar paper
pouting house out back
where he would go
to sit persecuting his memories
and pretend to recite scripture

he was a cross
between a cathartic
and a four tablespoon dose of castor oil
on the one hand
he had a personality
like one more worst ever Sunday homily
salved with tortured exegesis and admonition
and for dinner after that was over
a Hemphill Wells ladies upper crust social club
Waldorf salad with Mandarin orange segments
unsalady things mixed perfectly nasty
slathered together and stirred
up with goddam mayonnaise

and on the other
his own family said
he was so dull-witted the ghost
in his grandmother's attic on his mama's side
abandoned the refuge from boredom two weeks
after he moved in with her
to give him a second chance over there
she said If he inherited
his way of being from his daddy

it's amazing that man
had enough spism in the bedroom
to even foster that child
which led to many theories
and rumors of parenthood

when he got old enough
to be a candidate for any form of complex
he became self-absorbed and convinced
the entire South Plains
saw the new star in the east
as his advance birth notice
cleared out seats for him
on the fifty yard line
at Texas Tech stadium
despite the mounting evidence
to the contrary in its
steady pile of accumulation

to any form of suggested self-correction
advice or criticism he would say
he was ambiffilant
to ever bit of it
a self made man
who didn't answer to nobody

thus he waxed in his youth

Anon when time came
for contemplation of the Rubicon
he cast about to survey
the available picked-over lot
for the highest ranking suitee
offering elevation on the Garza County social ladder
then settled upon B. L. Wayburn's daughter

with the big ears and turned up nose
courted her for a period of one month
hence made his way to the Wayburn homestead
to offer his hand in marriage
on a Monday evening when
the Wayburne Pig Cafe closed at four

stated his intentions clearly
to B. L. Wayburn who listened thoughtfully
then asked Odus Millard
if he had in actuality proposed marriage to his daughter
Odus Millard said Nosir that's a fact
I thought it would be appropriater
to present myself and my case to you
before I decided on situational permanence
and B. L. Wayburn said Which air case?
Odus Millard said The matter
of keeping your daughter in a manner
to which she is become accustomed
and B. L. Wayburn said Whar?
Odus Millard said I was thinking
perhaps of a partnership in the cafe

B. L. Wayburn said Son
you have no more idea of business
than a hog does of the sacrament
it aint enough money in that cafe
to keep one family in a prosperous manner
to which they'd like to become accustomed
much of a less two
what ever possessed you
to think of such a thing?
Odus Millard said It was only
the comfort and welfare of your daughter
that was ever of my prime concern
and the fact that she was nearing
the state of spinsterdom
and in a honest manner of speaking

is not ezactly a candidate
to be the Maypole Harvest Queen
nevertheless I believe we could
find happiness under the right fixed conditions

after which B. L. Wayburn said Boy
you may exactly be right
but I have to inform you
in an honest manner of speaking
that you are not exactly an agricultural genius
and you are damsure not
a candidate for hellofaman of the year
so it might even out in a long run
I do not know her attitude toward you
but I do know there is no accounting for taste
and I've said once
and I'll now say it twicet
a woman can only love a thing
if she can pity it
and then run over it
so you might be just what she's destined for
but after that unless you can frycook and haul garbage
you're on your own as far as my cafe goes
with that as my blessing
and my fervent hope
this will be a childless relationship

and in lieu of a better offer
they had a private wedding
three weeks later on a Thursday
in Via Acuna, Mexico

Odus Millard found quickly
the terrible misunderestimation
of his spouse who was brimful
with spit and vinegar

and when provoked had two screams
of retribution and social commentary
one of which was imperative punctuational
almost preacherly in deliverance
and the other recreative and ebullient
as if she'd opted for celibacy and made the decision to give up
chamomile tea, honeygar and Baptist salvation permanently
often expressing her loathing of mankind
within the same outpour of libationous scream
on or without demand

while he intimidated
could barely come to the cusp
of being self-sanctimoniously
larded with piffle
memorizing three scriptures by heart
beginning with Ephesians 5: 23 and 4
always forgetting the second to approach
climax with a grand finale of 1 Peter 3: 5
which he recited to her deaf ears
on any occasion deemed beatific

and soon learned his proper position
in their formal relationship
trailing behind her like ballast
apparently unaware of his universal appraisal
of being neither useful nor ornamental
in their familial pecking order
having learned the intrinsic Texas personality value
of snorting and harking so that
he quickly became a veritable sputum machine
always a step and a half in arrears
so that Bus Pennel could say
She never had no need of a pugdog
but Billy Klogphorne said
Odus had the reminiscent waddle of a
fucking duck on a tether

Thirty years passed without a single
waxing moon in their marriage
during which time his wife in name only
became assistant and in his words co-conspirator
to her father's Wayburne Pig Cafe
long after Odus had been permanently banished
for telling seven year old Leon Teasdale
to Wipe that smirk off your silly assed face in here
upon which Eva Lou Teasdale burst
into a litany of tears and sorrow and trembling
provoking B. L. Wayburn to tell Odus
Goddam boy caint you see he's got a harelip?
upon which Odus said Well I never noticed
I thought he was mocking me

he would sit on the raised wall bench
at the poolhall all day and argue
with anybody who was willing
over anything that was accomodable
including whether garbage was picked up
on a Tuesday or Thursday at the Algerita Hotel
or the merits of blue or white cue tip chalking
though he never once played a game of snooker
to the private intimacies of public education employees
and the utter worthlessness of married life
shifting subsequently to his interest in politics
where in the preliminaries
he was defeated on three occasions
to be the Democratic nominee for mayor
then in unmitigated oratorical anger, wrath and spiteful venom
unbeknownst to anyone save the bathroom mirror
he revenged himself upon humanity
switching to the Republican regime
and for the rest of his life
regardless of never casting a single electoral vote
abode no Democrat in his presence
finally withdrawing countenance to all men
who did not vote straight ballot God's Own Party

seriously narrowing the candidacy list
of potential friendship or commerce with any person
holding the social status to which he aspired

until finally everyone he knew by name died
and unable to place names with recognized faces
he gave up on remembering faces
withdrawing completely into his own anger

thus began the slow process
of wasting away, rectitude and atrophy

during which period of life
coughing fits
kept him awake deep into the night
until his wife drove him to the hospital
one morning in her bathrobe and told him
Get the hell out of this car and go see
somebody about this shit
where Dr. Tubbs told him smoking cigarettes
was going to kill him and gave him
an illustrated pamphlet on cancer
which he read carefully perusing the vivid pictures
of tumors and polyps and rotting lung tissue
then threw into the garbage can beneath the kitchen sink
and vowed eternal abstinence
his wife said You're quitting smoking?
he said Hell no
that's the last damn book
I'm ever going to read
and as far as she knew he kept his word

it was then he built the tar paper
pouting house with the dirt floor
which became his sanctum sanitorium
in a world he no longer acknowledged
or pretended to belong to

His wife said
He was a lifelong slow waker
liked to sit with his coffee
all alone and stare out the window
at the horizon
for as long as he possibly could

when asked to do any chore
or pressed for the merest conversation
he'd say he preferred
to contemplate the scriptures
no one ever saw him read
in solitude

until he had his heart right
with the god she knew
he didn't believe in
as his chosen remembrance
out in that cross-the-tracks shanty
she planned to tear down tomorrow

from the *Pipe Springs Bugle,* November 17, 1956, page 4

ODUS MILLARD

Closed casket graveside services were held on Thursday for Odus Millard, date of birth unknown, who apparently died on Tuesday when he was found in the shed behind his house after not coming in for supper by his wife of unknown causes though it is known he claimed to be inflicted with black lung disease not caused by or incidental to cigarette smoking. His family had no knowledge of previous employment in the mining industry or extended employment at any other workplace. He attended high school in Matador, it is unknown whether he graduated. He is survived by his wife who asked that her name not be used in this obituary. The marriage produced no offspring. B. L. Wayburn announced that free coffee would be offered at the Wayburne Pig Cafe to anyone who stated that he or she was a personal friend of the deceased.

Yet Another Reason

on Billy Jack Johnston opposing the gravelling
of city streets before the season of wind

He needs a jackass
to kick him in the mouth
and by god
I may just do it

From sidebar minutes of the monthly
Town Board Meetings
16 April 1957

Found Poem

from the Police Blotter
Pipe Springs Bugle, July 21, 1957, page 4

On July 17th at 12:36 a.m., Officer
Deputy Sheriff Junior Shepherd
pulled over Aleptis Smallwood
allegedly of Turkey, Texas, after
which he subsequently identified
himself as the driver of a 1951
Chevrolet Bel Aire automobile in
question and then the vehicle was
designated with an improper license
plate and false registration which was
then classified as the property of his
alleged brother Eucalus Smallwood,
address unknown, which is a wanted
criminal and was then arrested for
bootlegging and false impersonation
of an automobile, presently confined
to the county jail pending clarification
of ownership and identity, trial
following at an unspecified date for
bootlegging before Judge J. A. Parker.

Three-Schlitz Monologue at the Dew Drop Inn

have you seen the car he drives?

—David Clewell, *The Low End of Higher Things*

1

Standing at the bar Bus Pennell said
Billy Clyde Patrice called this afternoon
when I said Hello he said
You feel like doing
some Christian neighborly helpout?
I knew it would be more trouble
than I wanted on any Friday good or bad
by the way he beseeched

I'd told Margaret a long time ago
if she ever asked Billy Clyde and Ihler
to go to church with her again
I was heading to Mexico for a week
and transferring to Coy's Assembly of God
right on that day
I didn't want to go in the first place
with her taking neighbors
it wasn't any way to get out of it
second song Don Clary had on his list
barely into the chorus
Billy Clyde said out loud
Who the hell wrote that thing?
Ihler tried to shush him he said
Listen to it Like a tree planted by the water
I shall not be moved
who would put a tree by the water
if he didn't want it moved?
couldn't never put down no tap root
first sandstorm would knock it over

flat on its ass
then when it came to prayer
before the sermon Charles Ivin's formuler
called for him admonishing rain
right after he'd blessed the sick and afflicted
Billy Clyde said I had enough
I aint staying no more
Ihler tried to grab his arm
hold him but he pulled aloose
said What kind of peckerhead
prays for rain on the first of October
when the bolls is already open?
picking season starts in two weeks
ever farmer on the South Plains
gone lose his crop if their Lord listens
to that pimple faced ignernt
you don't pray for rain now
that was a month ago
got up and walked out
Charles Ivins still reciting
in the wishes and needs section
of his resurrected prayer outline

2

Hello Billy Clyde I said
what kind of a problem is it today?
he said If it's not one damn thing
it's a dozen my mama always said
I caint get this car to crunk
I need yall to come give me
a jump or a starting push
I said All right neighbor
I'll do what I can
one way or anothern
then when I hung up I took a walk
back in my mind the first time

I ever saw Billy Clyde Patrice's car
I said What kind of a vehicle is that?
he said It uster be a blue one
now it's more of a green
bending to yallow like a foot mark bruise
on a fat womern's butt
might of been a Ford oncet
sorter of a Heinz 57 any more

hood off and a Crisco can's bail
hanging on a homemade tripod
a rubber siphon hose
with a clothespin bleed valve
dripping gasoline into the carburetor
he said It'll run but it won't go
hollered at Ihler sitting in the front seat
bellowing she was Gone be late
to close her mouth
he was talking here
said She hates ever where she's ever been
hates where she's going
and hates more where she's at
Would you just shut the hell up?
we'll get there on time
if we don't they'll play
a second feature at nine
we piddled with the drip line
half an hour listening to her moan
then found out the Crisco can
had elm leaves in it
choking off the siphon suck

he said Was it any chance
yall was going in to watch
the picture show up to town tonight?
it's posta be a real good one they say
I said No it hadn't crossed our minds
what was it that was playing?

he said he really didn't recollect
but they'd be happy to come along
if we went and keep us some company
turned out to be one of the worst
nights of our married lives
Billy Clyde hollered Shoot her to John Wayne
pointing his gun at that girl
Comanches captured as a baby
raised as their own In the head
No no John don't do it yelled Ihler
she's a innocent caint hep it
You shut your mouth Ihler he said
it aint none of your bidness
she's arredy spoilt where no
white man would ever have her anyway
shoot that half breed nephew in front of her too
he don't stand aside like you told him
I never liked his Jesus H. Christ
pretty boy looks in the first place
when the picture show was over
I wanted to slip out quick
they wouldn't have any part of it but
to stay and watch the cartoon and
prevues of the coming feature attractions
all the people walking up the aisle
staring at us so that for the first time
I knew what it was going to feel like
when I was a old man over forty
and then Margaret invited them
to come along to church with us
as her personal self-inflicted penance

3

went out to look
his battery dead as a Jerico Road truck smashed cat
generator belt rotted out and flopping

terminal poles corroded
like petrified bucking bull snotslobber gobs
he said Yall bring any jumper cables
mine is burnt to hell all ruirnt?

for once in my life my brain
wasn't stuck in compound spinning tires
I said Billy Clyde I don't believe
I might not have any
I'll go back to the house and see
what I can turn up
he offered to come along and help
I told him he better stay
hold down the fort and wait for the calvary
Ihler appeared to be teetering on a spasm clift
if he'd got in my truck there's no way
he wouldn't of seen my jumpers
laying under the seat on the floorboard
I knew if I hooked up to him
I'd probably burn up the cables
maybe all the wiring in both vehicles
my battery would wring itself out
be about worth as much as if
I put it on a stick of dynamite and lit the fuse
after I got him up to full charge
told him I'd already said I'd get him some help
one way or another
just hold tight till it comes

drove home and got Margaret
to call information and get me the number
of Ronnie Parker the new Campbellite preacher
who said in his first sermon
his number one priority was to seek out
all the strayed off flock last preacher'd passed over
bring them back into the fold
I called told him
Brother Parker it's a poor unfortunate

former member I'm pretty sure
of God's true church
is in sincere need of Christian help
told him where Billy Clyde and Ihler lived
that if he didn't have any jumper cables
he could go by Deacon Sonny Latham's place
his was on the left hand wall in his garage
which he always left the door of open
during the day when he was out working cattle
I was purdy sure he wouldn't mind
that much if he borrowed them
and I was real sorry I was too far away
to be able to be of any practical help to him
but that them Patrices would be surely appreciative
of his Christian brotherly love assistance

told Margaret I had to run into town quick
get some errands worked on and possibles bought
if anybody needed me maybe call
Noahie at the feed store
I might be still there
drove straight here
it aint no listing in the dry half of the county
for a bootlegger beer joint in the flats
the new preacher hasn't lived here
long enough to know where it's at
I bet five dollars Margaret's put the phone
off the hook after the first seven calls
from Billy Clyde Patrice
I do hope that preacher has some warranty
left on his station wagon

tonight after Margaret's through
talking to me about it
I will tell the Good Lord Brother Parker
probably deserves at least
a one slot upgrade in whatever place
he's got acoming in the afterlife

and that Yessir I'll be obliged
taking another step backwards and wind up
permanently here for the everlasting with gentlemen
I know and love like the Good Book tells us to
standing at the bar with a coldbeer in hand
down at the Dew Drop Inn

for the Clewell clan

Found Poem

*Written on the end page of a Gideon Bible
in a half-price motel room containing a dysfunctional
television set in Van Horn, Texas*

4
~~3~~ ₍ₙ₎things to make life better

1. drank at least a glass of water ever day
2. keep your dogs fed
3. say your priors when you think of it
4. dont think no main thoughts even about your enemyes
5. be carefull how you talk in front of a mans waf and his dog

p.s. did you ever notice that dog spell backwards was God
Think about that some time

Harold Rushing's Prayer While Shaving

as overheard by his son Mike

Lord, I've said this
to Suetta and the boys

but it occurs to me
that I need to repeat this upward
in a beseeching manner

I swear, Sir, I did not design
this farm on purpose

as a non-profit institution

Incident at Thompson Slough

1

Ollie McDougald said all things considered
which he admitted free and clear he hadn't
next time he'd walk or hitchhike
and if that nephew of his by marriage
on his wife's side ever sat out in his pickup
half of a Monday night listening to the radio
with that one girl in the front seat
running down the batteries
until nothing wouldn't crunk that morning
he'd separate his habits from his ideas
with a two by four or a broke off shovel handle

if he lived to be a hundred and four
he'd never figure out how he let that boy
talk him into getting on a bicycle
with a John Deere teeshirt and a basket on front
to bring the groceries back from the store
on double S & H Greenstamps day
he hadn't rode no bicycle for forty years
but that boy said it's one of those things
you never forget how to do like swimming
or making love to something firm and young
he didn't think to tell him
he never learned how to do moren dog paddle
and he knew for a fact he'd forgot
anything else about the othern
a real long time ago

there he was wobbling down the road
on the way to Piggly Wiggly
boy said he was too tored
to offer to make the towntrip for him
it was only six miles mostly flat

he's sure it'd be okay and the doctor
said he oughta get some exercise anyway

2

It might have been a red letter day he said
except half a mile down the road
here came Coach Bing Bingham from the high school
in his freshwashed car that morning
taking it out to dry and show off said
What's that bicycle you're riding?
Ollie said It's my nephew's by marriage
on my wife's side
he said I can see that it's a red one
where you going to on it?
Ollie said to Piggly Wigglys if I can
make it that far before tonight
Coach Bingham said
Yall want a tow into town?
Ollie said Whar?
Coach said I got a rope in my trunk
we'll tie it to my bumper and on
them handlebars I'll give you a pull
you can coast in the whole live way
Ollie said Not too fast
I aint much of a good
on one of these no more
he said I'll go slow
you hang on and ride
tied the tow line up and got in
then before he started his car
got back out and brought Ollie
this coaching whistle on a loop string
put it around his neck and said
It'll be just fine but if something goes wrong
I don't see it in the carmirror
blown that whistle till I stop

got back in they started off slow
driving in to Piggly Wiggly grocery store
pulling Ollie McDougald on a red bicycle
with his 1957 black brand new production model
Bonneville Pontiac the football boosters presented him
as an incentive to beat Tahoka
shining from the fresh carwash
like diamonds stitched in a bull's butt

3

It was going a squatch better
than OIlie McDougald said he thought
he could have expected
until Clarence Ivie in his pickup
he'd put a new 357 engine in
with cherry bomb mufflers comes
down the road late to get home
in horrible trouble with his wife
because him and his boy
who'd just turned eight years old
at one minute after midnight that morning
in the third grade
named Jerry Don Ivie that fall
were supposed to go up to the store and buy her
Meadowlark butter to make pie crust with
while she finished boiling dewberries
but he heard down to Adolph's cafe on the way
the news that Artie Gill that morning
caught a bass nine pounds and twelve ounces
over to Justiceburg Lake he said
he had to see with his own eyes
before he'd believe it and since
he had his poles in the truckbed
maybe he'd cast out a time or two
let Jerry Don see if it was any
catfish biting on the bottom

which he thought was a real good idea
to celebrate his birthday with

both catching fish
almost a towsack full
two good sized bass and one catfish
Clarence had to help him on
upwards of four pounds
he thought he was pretty sure about
never did see Artie Gill's bass
but they were all talking about it
down to the lake so it must have been
true more or less at least
then he remembered that butter
said Uh oh Jerry Don
we better be getting back home
your mama's going to have her drawers
up her crack if we don't get to the store
went to his pickup
it was a potential tragedy
wouldn't turn over
all the electric flatlined
had to follow it down the wires
until he found a fuse blown dead
piddled through his jockey box
to see if he had anything might work
only thing that fit
was a .22 bullet out of his pistol
he put it in and said Well I'll be
when it worked and the pickup started

pulled out and drove to town
fifty five miles an hour
as an example to Jerry Don of the law of the land
until he came up on Coach Bingham
he'd played football for almost ten years ago
pulling Ollie McDougald on a red bicycle
with a towing rope

came up beside him with the window down
racked his cherry bomb mufflers
hollered Flip a booger on him Jerry Don
just at the same time that boy
pulled one loose and he did
right on the hood of Coach's shiny black car
said I got him Daddy
Coach Bingham hollered Damn you
Clarence Ivie yelled Not if you caint catch me
shifted up to second and peeled rubber
Ollie McDougald said Oh no

4

How could it be but just at that second
Deputy Sheriff Junior Shepherd down
to the four mile bridge cutoff under
the big shade tree taking his turn
showing Maudie Fay Rayburn how the inside
of the new two year old patrolcar looked
heard those cherry bomb mufflers
said By god I bet
that's Clarence Ivie in his pickup
she said Where's he at?
heard those tires squalling said
By god I bet he's racing that pickup
she said Racing it where?
sat up in time to see Clarence go by
on the road like it was Indianapolis
jumped over the seatback
took out the microphone hollering
Sheriff Floyd Sheriff Floyd set up a road block
it's Clarence Ivie coming in to town
past four mile going eighty miles an hour
I'll be in pursuit said Maudie Fay
you have to get out
I'll come back and get you pretty soon

she said Get out where?
Sheriff Floyd called back
on the radio said Come again Junior?
here came Coach Bingham
wide open in his shiny black '57
Pontiac Bonneville honking like a skein of geese
leading in the Second Coming

Sheriff Floyd Sheriff Floyd he hollered
It's Coach Bingham going
wait a minute
Lord God amitey
it's Ollie McDougald on a red bicycle
90 miles a hour blowing a whistle
trying to pass
get out Maudie Fay
you have to get out NOW
Right here? she said
leaned over the seat and opened the backdoor
pushed her out on the ground
I have to go to work he said Right now
she said you sonofa Bye said Junior
in the office Sheriff Floyd said
Oh Lord I'm afraid Maudie Fay might of
unscrewed Junior's brains out this time
went out to his patrolcar to go see

5

Two miles outside town Coach Bingham
caught up to Clarence Ivie
sat on his bumper
horn wide open
Ollie McDougald blowing his whistle
like a jet airplane and Junior Shepherd
coming off the gravel road on to the pavement
with his red lights and siren screaming

maybe it was the heat inside that pickup cab
or an act of God just then
that .22 bullet went off loud
as a stick of dynamite
tore into the pickup seat up
to the ceiling right through
Clarence Ivie's left testicle

Jerry Don Ivie said he couldn't remember
exactly what it was his daddy said
it all happened quick
and the noise was loud
he remembered the pickup going
into the ditch and him thinking
Daddy, Mama's going to be real mad

6

Clarence Ivie's pickup bounced off the road
into the right hand borrow pit
spun twice and jumped the off side cleft
high centered with the rear wheels
spinning loose gravel forty five feet back
onto the pavement
cherry bomb mufflers backfiring
like 4th of July

Coach Bingham sideslid left axle deep
then sank halfway into Thompson Slough
up to his doors before he could imagine
what happened bellowing like a tornado
said he had to crawl through the window
out on the cartop to see where he was at

Ollie McDougald's red bicycle
turned into a launched skyrocket
over Coach Bingham's Bonneville Pontiac

fifty feet out into muck
before they ceased partnership
that whistle blowing so hard
his face looked like two muskmelons
stuck on his cheeks
bicycle landed upside down in a juniper
front wheel a windmill spinning
like an Olympic champion
Ollie bellyflopped in gumbo
slid twenty more feet up onto tule grass
rolled over thinking he was blind for life
or dead in black hell
until he wiped off the mud
not a single bone broken
or a bloody nose for a souvenir
said he had to pull the whistle up
by the string from where he swallered it

Deputy Sheriff Junior Shepherd
screamed on the scene one minute and
fifty six seconds later
eighty two miles an hour
locked his brakes and skiddered sideways
a quarter mile down the pavement
sank the front end of his patrolcar
into the slough
crawled out the back window and hollered
Yall all under arrest
don't you move any of you
I got reaforcements acoming

Cletis Graves puttered up from his place
with Maudie Fay Rayburn on his tractor fender
picked up on the road if she sworn
she wouldn't tell nobody
Jerry Don Ivie screeching
like a banshee when his daddy
pulled down his pants and saw blood

all over his pecker down his legs
said Oh god I'm bleeding to death
holding his privates fainted dead away
Sheriff Red Floyd pulled up
sat in his car looking out at the slough
didn't even recognize Ollie McDougald
so covered up with mud
said the only thing he could think of
was to wonder what the hell
was a bicycle doing with its tires
spinning upside down in a juniper tree
and how come Maudie Fay Rayburn's
wearing Junior Shepherd's policeman's hat
when the radio came on and the dispatcher
Sheila Morris said Sheriff Floyd
it's Darlene Ivie on the line saying
her husband and son aint come home
they posta be bringing her some Meadowlark butter
Junior Shepherd hollering
Yall under arrest
Coach Bingham yelling That little buggar
flipped a booger on my car
Ollie McDougald asking Am I dead?

Sheriff Floyd said Oh Lord Sheila
you better tell Darlene to go get in her car
and start it up
Clarence and her boy been involved
in a incident at Thompson Slough

7

He was posta be getting Meadowlark butter
Darlene Ivie said
Mama said Jerry Don Ivie
Maam said Sheriff Floyd
I'd just warshed that car all clean

said Coach Bingham
My car wouldn't crunk and I needed
groceries said Ollie McDougald
Mama said Jerry Don
I caint make no pie crust without
butter said Darlene
Maam your husband's in the ambulance
on the way to the hospital said Sheriff Floyd
They was going 90 miles a hour at least
I'll swear to it said Junior Shepherd
Mama said Jerry Don
Did he get my butter? said Darlene
Now look whatall happened said Coach Bingham
They're all under arrest said Junior Shepherd
Here take this you horse's ass said Maudie Fay
gave him back his hat
Mama said Jerry Don
WHAT! Darlene said Jerry Don
Mama Daddy shot off his balls said Jerry Don
Jerry Don I wished you wouldn't talk like that
said Darlene
Maam said Sheriff Floyd
Where is my Meadowlark butter? said Darlene
Ollie did you flown that red bicycle up in that tree
upside down like that? said Maudie Fay

8

Junior would you go get this womern
her Meadowlark butter? was what Sheriff Floyd said
that got Darlene Ivie calmed down
and Jerry Don in the car to take him home
so the wench truck could get close enough
to pull Coach Bingham's Bonneville Pontiac
out of the slough and Clarence Ivie's
pickup off the borrow pit ridge
paid Arlis Jamerson five extra dollars

county money to wade out and get
Ollie McDougald's nephew's by marriage
on his wife's side's red
bicycle out of the juniper tree
upside down Ollie said
he wouldn't never ride it no more again
and he didn't want no groceries today after this
double S & H greenstamps or not
washed his face off best he could
in slough topwater
Cletis Graves went on along after
nothing else was left to see
Junior Shepherd offered Maudie Fay
a ride in to town she said
she'd rather walk
Sheriff Floyd loaded the red bicycle
in the trunk of the patrolcar
Ollie and Maudie Fay Rayburn
in the back seat together
drove them to McDougald's
where they both got out
Maudie Fay said she'd be fine for tonight at least
on the way found out on the radio
Clarence Ivie lost one nut
they'd have to keep him over a couple of days
but wasn't otherwise mutilated
or incapacitated and Deputy Sheriff
Junior Shepherd knocked on the door
when she answered it said
Here's your butter Maam

9

Sheriff Floyd Sheila Morris said
from the dispatch office
It's Darlene Ivie on the line
wondering if anybody knows when Clarence

will be coming home and
if anybody thought
to get that towsack of fish
out of her husband's pickup
and bring it by to her house
so she can fix some supper

Big Bend Triptych

1

Cottonwoods

bent over the seep spring
like viejos
wondering what it was

the wind uncovered
and who put it there

a page
from an ancient myth
in need of translation

surely a miracle
to be understood
through the ceremony
of libation

2

Hot

morning sweats with fervor
Droplets
like sin offerings

evaporate into mirage puddles
as believable as salvation
or the serpent's memory
of the garden

Blistered sand
clean as a miraculous portrait
of the Guadalupe virgin
woven by windrift

patiently waits
the monsoon shatter
of pitchfork rain

3

The delicate balance

Santa Elena's shoulders
bunched together
above the quiet river

a dream pathway
for the waxing moon
to carve the letter
of el nombre de dios into sky

above the darkened world
as the river's nubbed teeth
gnaw the slot canyon subway
into granite silt

carrying the great
stone walls
grain by immaculate grain
to sea

Another Reason Why You Didn't Want Kristine Thornton to Talk During Town Board Meetings

called out to Billy Hill
during a smoke break

I saw that girl of yours
wearing short shorts downtown yesterday
Deacon Hill
she's so skinny I told my husband
I couldn't tell if them were her laigs
or if she was riding a chicken

From sidebar minutes of the monthly
Town Board Meetings
23 June 1959

Cannonball

Hebrews 12:1

1

Yellow Flag

Howard Dale Teaff was
a fast car driver
like his daddy Roy and brothers were
but he misunderestimated his timing
crossed the yellow line his daddy
always said was only cautionary
went out just like them
in a bottle rocket firecracker shower of glory
before he even had the opportunity
to hire on professional like they did
driving bootleg liquor
in from Big Spring
then racing in Lubbock and Hobbs
on Saturday nights

Charles O'Neill lived through
the accident because
they made him sit in the backseat
by himself so the other three
could talk personal that night up front
where he wasn't able
to get flung out and mashed over
Dr. Tubbs said he wasn't hurt or killed any
to speak of in a social manner
but came to the funeral
in a rented wheelchair to make
his memorial pronouncement
so the community wouldn't hold
his survival against him too much

when it was his turn to bear testimony
he said Old Cannonball
was probley my best friend on earth
and right before he went
into the barrowpit and everything
turnt into a blurt mess right up to
almost this ezact moment
the very last thing I remember hearing
him say from his own mouth
as his final words
was to Luther he said Here Junior
hold my beer
I'm gone try something
then the world stood on its head

friends of the family to enhance the service
hired Lucille Bullard
our professional mourner
to come and do a half performance
which was all they felt
they could contribute and afford
at that very moment she commenced
a low moan from the bottom of her throat
that raised hair on all present arms
up to a wattle shaker minor wail
leaning toward potential bawl

unknown to their plans
two high school sophomore girls
who had been known relations
of the non-blood-familial type
to Howard Dale
became simultaneously overfilled with grief
and extraordinary bereavement
from opposite sides of the churchhouse
joined in with matched competitive howls
writhed and bent over hairpulling
so effective not one person

in attendance could have described
any part of the eulogy
Reverend Coy Stribling delivered
his epiphany stolen
right out from under him
us all in a wonderment
at their God's mercy and judgment

2

Checkered Flag

At the graveyard
when the pallbearers placed the casket
on the runner bands
stepped back to take off
their boutonnieres and lay them
on top of Howard Dale Teaff's coffin
the two high school drag race sweethearts
and Lucille Bullard whose salary
for the ceremony did not include
a graveside sorrow rendition performance
together did an impromptu benefit
standing in a perfect isosceles triangle

started with a wail howl
like a band saw
splitting into silver highs
and sheet iron middle range lows
each taking a solo in a perfectly modulated
aria series of coloratura soprano
mezzo and alto dropping to counter tenor
then rejoining and rising
to perfect pitched harmonic crescendo
that could not have been more gloriously
conjoined if Georgie Wilson
director of our world famous

high school choir had color-coordinated
and personally directed it
garnering applause from
a considerable portion of the audience

after which Howard Dale's mama Merlene
seized the cameo moment for her appearance
approached her son's casket
laid an unpaid speeding ticket
among the scatter of white carnation boutonnieres
and said real low but so everybody
there as witnesses could hear
Oh Haard Dell I'm so sorry
your daddy and brothers couldn't be here today
Roy would have been so proud of you
and she patted the end of the coffin
his head wasn't on

walked over and got in her new
used insurance-car and drove
pretty fast some said
back to the Church of God of Prophesy
where bretheren had brought
a pot luck memorial communion
where she went in by herself
first in line
to sit down at the long table
with a black and white plaid plastic tablecloth
in the Sunday School room
and have her some supper
of fried chicken and mustard potato salad
two light bread dinner rolls with butter and jelly
with a side of boiled bacon collard greens
and a large offering of Mrs. T. L. Jones'
first prize blue ribbon county fair
sour cream raisin cobbler for dessert
to conclude the everlasting solemnities
her and her family's race all run

Wednesday Night Solemnities
at the Dew Drop Inn

After Jerry Lee Lewis jukeboxed
Great Balls of Fire
Ben Howell said he recalled
that time once upon
when he was this younger stallion
up in Alaska Yukon
one summer digging goldmines
with his daddy
them roaring borealases all over
sky red and yellow and green fore
great round balls like the Marfa lights
about that same time John Wayne
was out there making the Giant picture show
when him and his family drove through
and almost got to be in it as extras
in that cafe fist fight where
he got his butt whupped good
Ollie McDougald said Oh hell

you was borned too old to of ever
been in either place
you wouldn't know what no borealas or Marfa light
looked like if it bit you on the butt
R. B. McCravey said You no more
seen a morphodite or John Wayne
than you heard a fart
in a thunderstorm
Cleotis Ledbitter said I don't believe
it was John Wayne in that movie show
anyway that I remember
he said Oh yes he was
and I can prove it
I seen the saddle he rode on

nailed to a ceiling in a Mexican cafe
in Salado, Texas and a card on the wall
said so with my own eyes
Bus Pennel said I don't believe it
John Wayne he never got his butt whupped
that couldn't of been his saddle
Cephas Bilberry said We given
out awards for horrible liars

you'd be crowned King of the World
he said Nahuh I wouldn't neither
R. B. said Well then who?
he said Any one of yall is
horribler liars than I am
I learnt it from you anyway
I'm still in a stage of education
there's Reverend Coy Stribling I bet
could be considered
what about him preaching his vision
after he heard Jimmy Swaggert
on all-night radio from Del Rio
warning everbody to be getting ready
it's a coming soon
Coy taking up that special ordained collection plate
so they could put football field lights
around his churchhouse
he'd make a homemade picture show
of the Second Coming to put on Lubbock
Sunday morning Gospel Hour channel 7
if it happened to occur in the nighttime
he'd be up and praying with the Lord
in the garden raring to go
he had his mind pure focused on the everlasting
holding prayer meeting and admonition

right now tonight
without none of yall even being there
to accuse him of such a thing

what about that?
they all didn't say anything else
gave their prompt attention back
to the matter of coldbeer
and personal meditation
because that might have been true
Coy he had him some purdy good talent
built up in that arena
anybody could be right even Ben Howell
once in awhile

And One More Reason

*to Reverend Strayhorn when he protested
the new home-ec. teacher lecturing her students
on human reproduction*

You preacher people
with your Peterless
non-existent Pearly Gates
think all the rest of us
are somehow worried that
we're locked out forever

*from the sidebar minutes of the monthly
Town Board Meeting
25 February 1960*

Found Poem in Four Hands

from a gas station restroom stall in Ft. Stockton, Texas

Repent   Jesus is coming
      Soon

Remember the Alamo

Well get him this time to

You better be careful
      you going piss him off

A True Story of Courage and Bravery

or What Cleotis Ledbitter Said in the Wayburn Pig Cafe that Morning

I done something
just as brave and popular
as them churchhouse and war
and football stories
yall been telling
that might not all
be even true stories
I really did save my dog
and my wife
before she died anyway
of the thrombosis
from probly getting killed
and eat alive one night

camping in the mountains
up to New Mexico
my dog he started snarling
got up to see what was the matter
this bear
rattling in the flour sack
silverware and bread
and moon pies and
two cans of spam was in
outside on the ground
dog went straight through
the tent door
to get him
I had to help right then
my wife ascairt
hollering like Jesust
had come back
calling in his folds

I had on only
boots and bvd's
with a flashlight
grapt that sack up
hollered and waven it
all in the air
where he'd pourn it out
got our pies
eat them all up
but one in his mouth
I run that bear off
with only my dog
and that flour sack
saved his life
and my wife
from harm and injury
putting my flesh between
them and the bear
in the night
that is the gods' truth

I can prove it
I got a picture
of that dog up to the house
and the flour sack
in the drawer
I can get it out and show you
any time you want to see it
that's all they are to it
maybe that'll give yall
something else new to talk about
for a little while

God's Lion, God's Lyre

bruising the teats of her virginity

Ezekiel 23

Before he reached what he called
his personal maturity
found Jesus so he could become
a gospel preacher famous
all over our county
Flynn Poque was our designated
town rounder and self-proclaimed
Champion High Plains Lady Killer
which he officialized by signing
eight different girls' school yearbooks
his senior year
With fond memories, Buster Hymen
aka Flynn the Great aka Cherry Pop

news got out Bill Edwards
said he had his biggest rush on shotguns
at his hardware store
he usually didn't see until
about every seventh year on average
before quail and duck season
four got special rock salt shells
Charles Huffman bought double ought
made such a threat of killing and mayhem
Sheriff Red Floyd had to go
down to the Dew Drop on a Thursday night
after calling first to let them know
it wasn't a bootleg raid
told him It wasn't worth it
going to prison over poaching
whitetrash out of season
town council sent a personal letter

advising his best interest
might be in patriotism
honoring his country in the military service

came back early
for the Convenience of the Army
started the rumor of foreshadowance
in the poolhall one day saying
he had the word Jesus
tattooed along the side of his peter
in Tijuana one night
so whatever he did with it
from then on was
in the name of the Lord

Billy Jo Hill who'd had a short tour of duty
with him a couple of years back said
She didn't believe in any part of it
because in her private personal opinion
he was a chickenshit coward
too ascairt to have gone through the ritual
but would have paid the price
of the tattoo for admission
to watch the squeamish sonofabitch
squirm and howl
in her own words

he saw the light and the paycheck
took over the Pentecostal Church
after Travis Mayfield quit and went
back to somewhere in Ecclesiastes they said
became a bench crammer of tithers who came
to see what he'd say this time
about God's pure unsullied church
grew a huge mane of hair
gave himself the title Great Lion of God
learned snake handling but not poison drinking
couldn't sew the jarlids shut, so it was dangerous

hired out at tent revivals
preaching and gospelsinging
accompanying himself on the guitar
which he called and had painted on it
King David's Virgin Lyre
drawing crowds from over twenty miles away
joined the Rotary Club and after three years
got elected chaplain and sergeant at arms
completely transmogrified and legitimized
a Legend in a bevy of innocent minds

✟

It was at Adolph's on a Saturday afternoon
during halftime of another unmemorable
Texas Tech football game
in a moment of rising personal community significance
interrupting a great spate of gossip
and retained personal hatred and unmitigated jealousy
Dan Cockrum put his divine gift of wisdom
and loquaciousness on public display
when he hit the bullseye once again precisely
reminding us concerning That boy
actually no longer a boy but an icon
of various and sundry interpretation
is one of our own, born, bred and nurtured by us
into his presence of being, furthermore
In the darkest toe of the muddiest cast aside
hand-me-down forgotten cowboy boot
in the trashiest cobweb strewn mudroom closet
of the most abandoned and forsaken line shack
in any reclaimed wilderness of identity
we will find our perfect memory and youth
if we search long and hard enough
through the mental pages of our own self-invention
and whoever's face we find
will just flat not be the one we expected
whether it's in the mirror or in front of us smirking

we are all of us of the same ilk and in this together
we best learn to live with it and each other

And by unspoken acclamation we reversed
grudgingly came to our senses
returned to our flowing libations of Pearl, Jax and PBR
accepting the inevitability of life's injustice
unpredictability of unanticipated
and perhaps unmerited success
and perpetuity of Red Raider defeat
acknowledged he was our town genius
the voice in the high plains whirlwind
we knew Dan Cockrum was exactly right
and that is why we should not build
private ownership roads into wilderness or the past
but allow it to lie undisturbed
breathing in the soil bank of its own redemption
pray fervently to our pantheon of barroom gods
to perpetuate wondrous beerhazes of nonrecollection
and furthermore let goddam sleeping dogs lie
and not hunt out and kill or mar the vanished memory
of our diminishing supply of homegrown treasures
lest we wake up one morning and find
we have become a community of sameness
without identity, our lives and worth
fallow shoals of sunsucked, desiccated sanddrift

and Another Reason

to Mack Wood, Kristine's former high school boyfriend
proposing opening soil bank land to cattle grazing

You're proof there's no such thing
as a circumcised cowboy
or one with a brain
you wouldn't have no place
to put your chew ever week
when your latest squeeze reminded you
to brush your teeth

from the sidebar minutes of the monthly
Town Board Meetings
14 December 1961

Prelude to an Autumn Elegy

Adolph's, Lake Hills, Texas

Then let us toast John Barleycorn
Each man a glass in hand

—Robert Burns

Over a frothy mug of dark ale
after singing along to the jukebox
Ballad of Davy Crockett
Scotty Sampson said It was
a gloaming thick as a tromp
of wet wool that day of remembrance

summerfat Herefords
trundled out of the bunched mesquite
streaming the dour hill country
like a bawling blood stain
crying for another year
almost gone

the gravity tug of southern warmth
respringing eternal in the feathered breast
of heaven's hurly burly undulations
great flocks of geese and cranes
ripping holes through the sky
with their cries of farewell

then like a flourish of Robbie Burns' pen
sunset ripened under Venus' beauty
a dying campfire smouldered
into the waft of fading cattle cries
sweet horse breath and creaking leather
beneath a moon of the hummingbird

So sang Scotty tonight to the oaks and rills
in a birthday backdrift
to that immaculate day sixty eight years past
when he A boy of twelve
rode bold upon a speckled horse
bringing the father's cattle in

Found Poem

*Dan Cockrum discovered and photographed during his summer
vacation on an outdoor restroom wall above the urinal beside
La Sagrada, Chimayo, New Mexico, which he blew up, framed
and hung in his bathroom above the toilet*

Forgive me Jesus

I am a sinner

~~Raphael Martinez~~

        Jesus would never forgive anyone
        who wrote his name on a shithouse wall

Overheard at Adolph's Coffee Counter

by Harold Rushing and Dan Cockrum:
Joe Bob Trammel Blowing Off Steam
After Town Board Meeting

By god
if I could
I'd write a book
about Kristine Thornton
some day

on the other hand
that might
be one
the world
could do without

Wheelis House: A Texas Tragedy

What can these shadowlike generations of man attain
but build up a dazzling mockery of delight
that under Their touch dissolves again?

--Sophocles, OEDIPUS REX

Dithyrambic Prologue

Fifteen minutes after the trial adjourned
the men's glee club gathered
at the Dew Drop Inn to tell each other
for the first time in a recurrent conversation
how it had been and whatall it meant
Clovis Ledbitter said We might of witnessed
the defining moment in our town's permanent memory
Ollie MacDougald said for his two cent's worth
It could go down as the most important
criminal trial in the history of Texas
but Dan Cockrum who was a printer
and the designated Gateway to the South Plains genius
because Mary Raephelt took her 4th grade classes
on field trips to his shop for forty years
where he demonstrated to a generation and a half
of young Tejas Republicans how he could type
sentences backwards on his printing press
and they would come out exactly right on the paper
which each and every one of us knew was a bona fide miracle
excepting Monroe Newberry who for the first time ever
could actually read it the turned around way
said You two speakers of the house chorus
are destined for immortal greatness because
neither of yall will ever be accused
of misunderestimating the situation at hand
and then he once again created the archetypal epiphany
in the exact center of the proverbial catharsis bullseye when he said

None of any of this might have happened
if Cloyd L. House hadn't shoved his way
into Wheelis's life buying him that damned car
he had to know no boy in his right mind would want
and we all knew he was spot dead accurate
when we put our minds back to that beginning
which set the entire sordid irreversible action in motion
over our copious libations of bootleg Pearl coldbrew

Strophe

Wheelis said By all rights
it should have been the happiest
time of his life but
whatever gods might be watching
over him had other ideas
he'd waited for two years
to get a brand new used car
he could get in and drag Main
chasing women any time he felt like it
but should have known it wasn't going to be
exactly what he anticipated
when his daddy showed him
what he picked out and his first clue
was two toned blue and orange

he even said What the hell
is that? his daddy said
It's a Ford
a good enough learner
Bus Pennel said Hope
you got a good buy on it
his daddy said Yessir
that is a sure enough fact
I bet that will get you Son
half a dozen new girlfriends

just waiting to see
what it looks like on the inside
Cephas Bilberry said he didn't think
it was that many blind wormen
in our part of the State
Wheelis's daddy huffed up said
You can take or leave it you don't like it
trade it in on one you want after you get a job
when you got the money to buy one then
took it out for a drive
with his mother and daddy supervising
the commencement of the world
caving in from the top down
didn't get two miles out of town
heard the sirens too late
highway patrol chasing bootleggers
hauling a beerload from Big Spring
over a ridgetop
Wheelis too green to know where to pull off
they plowed into that first new car
on his side of the road head on
like eight sticks of dynamite
mashed his Ford up
into a giant blue and orange plastic brillo pad
killed his mama on the spot
knocked his daddy into a coma
he held on to a week before he died
welded itself around Wheelis
where they had to cut his new used car
apart like a jigsaw puzzle
his clutch leg twisted around on itself
upwards of seven times
one of the firemen said they might
as well take it off with a chainsaw
or a cutting torch
but Dr. Tubbs did it proper in the hospital
bootlegger's car busted apart
slung them into the bushes

one dead and the other one run off
never did figure out who he was
all four doors flung out and trunk lid
blown half way to Tahoka
said it was enough beer on the road
all the fireboys could have
got down like Gideon and had a slurp
only two went ahead and did
all the rest drained in and ruint

Wheelis got a fatwife out of it
when one of the Shoemaker girls
being a nurse for the time being took to him
in the hospital where they got married
him still in bed by Reverend Coy Stribling
until she found out the insurance
was not going to be up to her prior expectations
covered his doctor bills and an artificial leg
that never did fit him where
he could walk on it more than a little ways
without the blister pain on the stub
putting him back on the furniture
until the State finally set him up with a new one
that worked More or less he said
in a hobbling manner
with a used walking cane
he got from Noah Stone's Feed Store
for fifty cents after the FFA livestock show

bills piled up
after his new wife quit her job
found out she couldn't draw unemployment
because she hadn't been fired yet
bank had to foreclose
on his daddy's house he inherited
before she ran off and left
put all his useless belongings in storage
sold the rest over the radio and a yard sale

took all the money with her
left Wheelis laying on a ratty couch
and a foot stool to prop his good leg on
not even a T.V. in a twelve year old used
twenty two foot trailer house
with one bedroom
she bought from her brother on credit
under Wheelis's name
parked under an elm tree
out by the airport no planes ever used
moved to Tahoka and got a job
at the Curl Up and Dye Hair House
running errands and cash register
and the next week
his dog took off and went
down the road toward Two Draw
never saw him again

Antistrophe

then the storage company
auctioned his belongings
because he didn't have
any money to keep up the rent
Charles Huffman said he
Seen this barbeque grill
looked like it might have some work
left in it he paid two dollars for
took it home and put it out back
in the yard under a tree
when he opened it in the summer
to see if he could make it cook
about had a brain spasm
It was a laig laying there inside
on top of the grill
like it was waiting to be supper

said after he got through being ascairt
took it in the house
kept it in the closet
except when he needed it to spook the kids at night
to make them stay in their bedroom
until his wife's mother came for dinner
when he put it on a table plate
like it was fixed to eat
she didn't come back any more
after that for a long time

then he got the second best idea
of his life after getting his kids
to sell Grit newspaper and White Rose Salve
and Chapstick tubes for piles
started up a Halloween spookhouse show
in his garage with that leg as the feature attraction
charged a nickel for kids under nine
a dime up to twelve and then fourteen
and a quarter for adults
said People come from all over
the world to see it with a golf ball
painted like Bus Pennel's eye tore out
viennie sausages and spaghettis
with tomater sauce and dog hair
every year spread the rumor
the National Museum in Warshington
loaned him John Dillinger's pecker
in a jar of pickled alcohol
that somebody said he was pretty sure
might be in there
and a womern's privates that was pig livers
and a kidney with some chitlins
in a Mason jar with pickle juice
you had to ask about special
if you were a certified adult
it was something not everybody got to see
one year there was a line half a block long

when Kim Pierce sold tickets
in a dress made for an elf
she slopped out of all four ways
when she bent over to tear them off the roll
and Ella Mae Blodgett stood
behind the leg asking customers
to Please don't touch it
it's fresh and aquivering
and she'd shake to prove it

Wheelis found out about it
went to see the Horrer Show
saw his used first artificial leg laying there
under a farrowing pen spotlight
went straight up to Charles Huffman
said That's my laig you got
Charles said No it's not it's mine
Where'd you get it at? said Wheelis
I bought it at the auction said Charles
I got a Bill of Sale for it to prove it
Wheelis begged him to give it back
for an hour in front of the customers
even said it was a gift to him from his run off wife
and the only memory of her left
it was real precious
Charles said No
Wheelis called in on the radio
and then the newspaper
four letters to the Editor
to take his case to the public
said That leg was his private personal property
that should of never been took away from him
while he was being incapacitated
and reduced to beggary for the rest of his life
any act of decency would give it back to him
Charles said No
it's become a major aspect
of my financial income

I caint let it go
without substantial recompension
it might be worth upwards of one thousand dollars
even more if Hollywood found out about it
and told Vincent Price
he might come and make a picture show out of it

Wheelis got an appointment
went to Judge Parker
told his story from the beginning
bawled in appropriate places to enhance his plea
so much that Judge Parker
called Charles Huffman in to intercede
he brought a valid Bill of Sale
marked $2 Paid in Cash
Judge Parker said Isn't there any way
we can negotiate this?
Charles Huffman said he didn't know
why Wheelis wanted it for
he already had a new one
Wheelis said It was like it was a part of him
that had been tore out of his life
Charles Huffman said he'd think about it
but was inclined to the negative

Epode

finally after two months
of Wheelis coming to the court house
every day sitting outside his office
or in the court room
telling anybody who would
or wouldn't listen about injustice
Judge Parker called them both in to court
for a special trial to resolve the issue
in a private session

so crowded with everybody
who had any way to get there
it was standing room only
to see what might happen

went on for an hour back and forth
with the Bill of Sale even passed around
the court room for proof
then Charles Huffman said
after Wheelis cried in the witness stand
where he swore himself in to tell
the whole honest truth
Out of the goodness of my heart
I am willing to offer Wheelis
joint custerdy of the laig
but he has to agree I get it back
a month in advance to set up my exhibits
in a productive manner
which is by the first of October
Judge Parker said to Wheelis
Would that satisfy you?
Wheelis said What if I wanted it in that month
so I could set me up a Hore House
and make some money out of it?
you wouldn't let me do that I bet
so do I have another choicet?
Charles Huffman and Judge Parker
both said at almost the same time
No

Wheelis House said
I want to dress the court
and after that I won't say no more about it
for the rest of my life ever
Judge Parker said You go right ahead then
we will listen real careful and then we'll be done
Wheelis said It aint no real justice for the little man
like Jesust said If it don't kill you

it will make you stronger
and it's about put me in the graveyard
Irby Metcalf said almost out loud
That wasn't Jesus it was Quannah Parker the Comanche Chieftain
with blue eyes at the battle of Adobe Walls
my granddaddy was there and heard him say it
This here said Wheelis is the saddest day of my life
I've done lost everything
my car
my diddy
my house
my barbeque grill
my mama
my wife
my dog run off
and now my laig

this is all the injustice
I was ever warned might come
and there's nothing I can do about it
my diddy told me when I was a baby
he was in the war where
he fought and died for his country
so men might have the rights to their privates
and now mine is being took away
where I don't have no control
or opportunity for financial annunciation
using what is rightly mine to get it
but this is the justice I have
and there's nothing I can do
but accept the best offer coming
my wife won't even be here
to testify on my behalf
I'm afraid my dog and my laig
are both gone for good
in a permanent manner of speaking
I have been abandoned of everything
and none of this might of happened

if my diddy hadn't bought
that damn blue and arng Ford
from his brother for bail money
which is a lesson to all of us
life is a line of dominos stacked up
waiting to go down
don't nobody else ever knock that first one over
after that it's all too late and nobody
will ever care or feel one bit sorry for you over it
that's my story

Judge Parker said
That was well done Mr. House
that is your story and I'm sticking to it
I declare joint custody in the matter
of the artificial leg in question
to be granted to Mr. Wheelis House
at any time he wishes to possess it
under the stipulation that it be returned
to Mr. Charles Huffman
no later than the first of October
in order to be set up in his exhibit
in a productive manner
for the entire month of October
is that acceptable to you Mr. Huffman?
Charles said Yessir your Honor
with maybe once in awhile on a Thanksgiving too
when the in-laws might be acoming for dinner
Judge Parker said Is that acceptable
to you Mr. House?
Wheelis scrunched his shoulders
but finally said Well okay then
Judge Parker said That said
this matter is hereby resolved
I declare this case permanently closed
and this court adjourned

Exode

and the men hurried to their cars
to get to the Dew Drop Inn
so they could tell each other
their side version of what happened
which might have been the end
of the story until all Wheelis's teeth
rotted and had to be pulled
and he bought a set of used teeth that never fit
where he couldn't eat ever again anything he liked
we all got to hear about it
when the opportunity presented itself
except he turned around and stared
at the people leaving the court room
bawling like a baby
until almost the last one was left
when he pulled out his handkerchief
blew his nose all into it
and threw it on the floor
said That is a symbol
of my opinion of Justice
and then he and his good artificial leg
hobbled out of the courthouse
with his feed store walking cane
into a bluebonnet sky world
where nobody was awaiting

Coda: Midnight Reflection

Starlight   River   Campfire   Coldbeer
"Endless Forms Most Beautiful"

In your tradition
where do we come from?

We come from the stars

You mean like God or gods
in the stars?

Nope

What then? Animistic spirits
flying saucers
myths and tales?

Amino acids in the meteorites
Building blocks of evolution
white guy

don't you read any science
in all that poetry?

for Michael Lacapa
Apache Hopi Tewa Storyteller
Vaya con dios, amigo

Acknowledgments

Thanks to the following publications in which
many of these poems first appreared:

By William Kloefkorn:

Paddlefish: "Sitting Next to a Young Woman Who Plays
Classical Violin"; "Reflection"; "Loves"

Omaha World-Herald: "Feathers"

Sewanee Review: "Early November 2008"; "Song in Praise of the
Beginning"

Flintlock: "Ashokan Farewell"; "Not the Same Reader Twice"

Sugar House Review: "Angelology"; "Sunday Morning on the
Patio"; "Sundown Syndrome"

New Letters: "Malaise"; "Sounds"

Chrysalis: "Saturday, Early April"

By David Lee

Connotations, Paddlefish, Red Thread Gold Thread
and Woodworks Press, where poems
in this collection first appeared.

About the Authors

William (Bill) Kloefkorn, professor emeritus of English at Nebraska Wesleyan University and the State Poet of Nebraska (since 1982) was born in Kansas in 1932, and died while this book was in preparation to go to press. He was the author of more than twenty collections of poetry, two short story collections for adults and one for children, and four memoirs. Although Kloefkorn's career was steadfastly academic in nature—before coming to Nebraska Wesleyan, he taught high school and at Wichita State University—Kloefkorn did, in fact, win the 1978 Nebraska Hog-Calling Championship, a fact which may explain his close friendship with former hog farmer poet David Lee.

Called a "modest Midwestern writer," Kloefkorn will always be remembered as a poet of the Great Plains. From prairie flowers to tractor accidents to wild weather, Kloefkorn's remarkably accurate eye and ear root us to particular moments in particular places. As *Booklist* put it: "It takes a rare and gifted writer to seamlessly transport the reader through the devastating fury of rumbling tornadoes and the delectable freshness of romantic awakenings."

David Lee was raised in West Texas, a background he has never completely escaped, despite his varied experiences as a seminary student, a boxer and semi-pro baseball player (the only white player to ever play for the Negro League Post Texas Blue Stars) known for his knuckleball, a hog farmer, and a decorated Army veteran. Along the way he earned a Ph.D., taught at various universities, and recently retired as the Chairman of the Department of Language and Literature at Southern Utah University.

Lee was named Utah's first Poet Laureate in 1997, and has received both the Mountains & Plains Booksellers Award in Poetry and the Western States Book Award in Poetry. Lee received the Utah Governor's Award for lifetime achievement and was listed among Utah's top twelve writers of all time by the Utah Endowment for the Humanities. He is the author of fifteen books of poetry. In 2004, *So Quietly the Earth* was selected for the New York Public Library's annual "Books to Remember" list.

Wings Press was founded in 1975 by Joanie Whitebird and Joseph F. Lomax, both deceased, as "an informal association of artists and cultural mythologists dedicated to the preservation of the literature of the nation of Texas." Publisher, editor and designer since 1995, Bryce Milligan is honored to carry on and expand that mission to include the finest in American writing—meaning all of the Americas, without commercial considerations clouding the choice to publish or not to publish. Technically a "for profit" press, Wings receives only occasional underwriting from individuals and institutions who wish to support our vision. For this we are very grateful.

Wings Press attempts to produce multicultural books, chapbooks, Ebooks, CDs, DVDs and broadsides that, we hope, enlighten the human spirit and enliven the mind. Everyone ever associated with Wings has been or is a writer, and we know well that writing is a trans- formational art form capable of changing the world, primarily by allowing us to glimpse something of each other's souls. Good writing is innovative, insightful, and interesting. But most of all it is honest.

Likewise, Wings Press is committed to treating the planet itself as a partner. Thus the press uses as much recycled material as possible, from the paper on which the books are printed to the boxes in which they are shipped.

As Robert Dana wrote in *Against the Grain*, "Small press publishing is personal publishing. In essence, it's a matter of personal vision, personal taste and courage, and personal friendships." Welcome to our world.

WINGS PRESS

Colophon

This first edition of *Moments of Delicate Balance*, by William Kloefkorn and David Lee, has been printed on 60 pound EB natural paper containing a high percentage of recycled fiber. Titles have been set in Papyrus type, the text in Adobe Caslon type. All Wings Press books are designed and produced by Bryce Milligan.

On-line catalogue and ordering available at
www.wingspress.com

Wings Press titles are distributed to the trade by the Independent Publishers Group
www.ipgbook.com
and in Europe by
www.gazellebookservices.co.uk